Visual Science Encyclopedia

Computers and the Internet

▲ This "tartan"-looking image is a closeup of a computer screen. It shows individual pixels, each carrying information about a single color. When it looks from a distance, the eye merges these color blocks into continuous tones.

How to use this book

Every word defined in this book can be found in alphabetical order on pages 3 to 47. There is also a full index on page 48. A number of other features will help you get the most out of the *Visual Science Encyclopedia*. They are shown below.

Here you will find the first word defined on any left-hand page.

Here you will find the last word defined on any right-hand page.

Each word is shown in bold so it is easy to find.

Other words defined in the book are highlighted in bold.

Each new letter of the alphabet is clearly marked to help you find the word you are looking for quicker.

Illustrations for some words complement the text and provide further information on a topic.

Plus, many entries point to related words of interest.

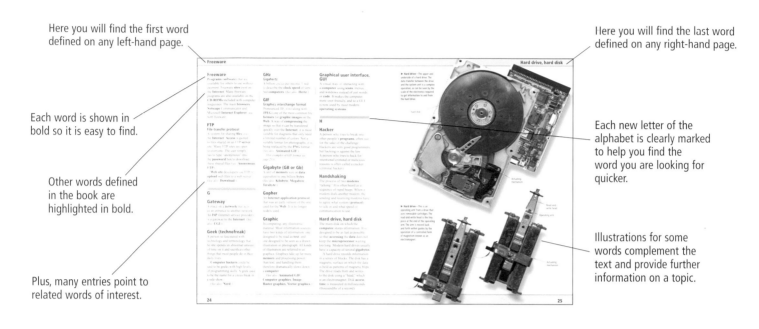

Acknowledgments

Grolier Educational
First published in the United States in 2002 by Grolier Educational, Sherman Turnpike, Danbury, CT 06816

Copyright © 2002
Atlantic Europe Publishing Company Ltd.

Author
Brian Knapp, BSc, PhD

Art Director
Duncan McCrae, BSc

Senior Designer
Adele Humphries, BA, PGCE

Editors
Lisa Magloff, BA, and Mary Sanders, BSc

Illustrations
David Woodroffe

Designed and produced by
EARTHSCAPE EDITIONS

Reproduced in Malaysia by
Global Color

Printed in Hong Kong by
Wing King Tong Company Ltd.

Library of Congress Cataloging-in-Publication Data
Visual Science Encyclopedia
     p. cm.
     Includes indexes.
     Contents: v. 1. Weather—v. 2. Elements—v. 3. Rocks, minerals, and soil—v. 4. Forces—v. 5. Light and sound—v. 6. Water—v. 7. Plants—v. 8. Electricity and magnetism—v. 9. Earth and space—v. 10. Computers and the Internet—v. 11. Earthquakes and volcanoes—v. 12. Heat and energy.
     ISBN 0-7172-5595-6 (set: alk. paper)—ISBN 0-7172-5596-4 (v. 1: alk. paper)—ISBN 0-7172-5597-2 (v. 2: alk. paper)—ISBN 0-7172-5598-0 (v. 3: alk. paper)—ISBN 0-7172-5599-9 (v. 4: alk. paper)—ISBN 0-7172-5600-6 (v. 5: alk. paper)—ISBN 0-7172-5601-4 (v. 6: alk. paper)—ISBN 0-7172-5602-2 (v. 7: alk. paper)—ISBN 0 7172 5603 0 (v. 8: alk. paper)—ISBN 0-7172-5604-9 (v. 9: alk. paper)—ISBN 0-7172-5605-7 (v. 10: alk. paper)   ISBN 0-7172-5606-5 (v. 11: alk. paper)—ISBN 0-7172-5607-3 (v. 12: alk. paper)
     1. Science—Encyclopedias, Juvenile. [1. Science—Encyclopedias.] I. Grolier Educational (Firm)
QI21.V58 2001
503—dc21
                          2001023704

Picture credits
All photographs are from the Earthscape Editions photolibrary.

This product is manufactured from sustainable managed forests. For every tree cut down, at least one more is planted.

A

Abandonware

Computer software such as a game that the owner no longer wants to use or to make money from. It is often then made available by someone else as **freeware**, which can be **downloaded** without charge.

Abbreviations used in chat

To make it faster to **chat** online using a **keyboard**, a set of abbreviations has come into common usage.

Some abbreviations are given in the table below.

Accelerated graphics port

A **chip** in a **computer** that allows 3D **graphics** to be displayed quickly on ordinary **PCs**. It uses the computer's main storage (**RAM**). The more **memory** the computer has, the faster the **image** will appear.

Access

Ability to get something that is needed. **Web** access involves having a connection to the World Wide Web through an **access provider**. (*See also:* **Password**.)

Access provider

An organization that provides you with **access** to the **Internet**. Internet access providers, also known as **ISPs** (Internet service providers), connect you to the Internet. Access providers usually have their own connection (point-of-presence —**POP**) on the Internet. A space provider (**SP**—also called a **virtual** host) is a company that provides space and management for **web sites**. Sometimes an ISP is also an SP.

Access time

The time it takes to retrieve **data**. It depends on the speed of the **computer chips** and also on the speed of the **device** that is storing the data, such as a **hard disk**. Access time to get data from the computer **memory** (**RAM**) is measured in nanoseconds (billionths of a second), while access time to a hard disk or **CD-ROM** is measured in milliseconds (thousandths of a second).

Acrobat

Software for **compressing files**, developed by Adobe Systems Inc. and now widely used on the **Internet**. It is particularly suitable for sending files containing pages of books because it will send both pictures and text in the same arrangements they were created in. The names of files compressed by Acrobat end in *.pdf*. (*See also:* **pdf** and **Portable device/document**.)

Acronym

The first letters of several words used to form a new word that is easy to remember. For example, the acronym for random access memory is **RAM**, and the acronym for beginner's all-purpose symbolic instruction code (a **computer** programming **code**) is **BASIC**.

Abbreviation	Meaning
ADN	Any day now
AFAIK	As far as I know
AFK	Away from keyboard
B4N	Bye for now
BAK	Back at the keyboard
BBIAB	Be back in a bit
BBL	Be back later
BFN	Bye for now
BG	Big grin
BRB	Be right back
BTW	By the way
CU	See you
CUL	See you later
CUO	See you online
DIKU	Do I know you?
DQMOT	Don't quote me on this
EMFBI	Excuse me for butting in
EOM	End of message
F2F	Face to face
FAQ	Frequently asked question(s)
FWIW	For what it's worth
FYI	For your information
GA	Go ahead
GIWIST	Gee, I wish I'd said that
GMTA	Great minds think alike
HAND	Have a nice day
HTH	Hope this helps

Abbreviation	Meaning
IC	I see
IM	Immediate message
IMO	In my opinion
IOW	In other words
JK	Just kidding
KWIM?	Know what I mean?
L8R	Later
LD	Later, dude
LTNS	Long time no see
NP or N/P	No problem
NRN	No response necessary
OIC	Oh, I see
OTTOMH	Off the top of my head
PANS	Pretty awesome new stuff
SF	Surfer-friendly (low-graphics web site)
STW	Search the Web
TAFN	That's all for now
THX	Thanks
TLK2UL8R	Talk to you later
TTFN	Ta-ta for now
TTYL	Talk to you later
TU	Thank you
UW	You're welcome
WUF?	Where are you from?
WYSIWYG	What you see is what you get

Active matrix display

A technology for creating the flat-panel liquid-crystal displays (**LCD**) in flat **computer monitors**, especially **laptop computers**, **palm computers**, and **WAPs**. They give a wider viewing angle than the cheaper passive matrix **displays**, but are still not yet as good as the cathode-ray displays found in desktop monitors.

Active server page

An **HTML** page that includes one or more scripts (small embedded **programs**) that are processed on a Microsoft-based **web server** before the page is sent to the user.

ActiveX

A small self-sufficient **program** (known as a component) that will run anywhere on the **Internet**, developed by Microsoft. The equivalent of a **Java applet**.

Adapter

A small piece of equipment that will allow a **device** with one kind of plug, pins, or voltage to run on a device that has different connections or voltage. Electronic adapters are built into adapter **cards** because adapting one electronic device to run in a different piece of **hardware** often requires special **circuits**, not just a new plug and socket.

ADC
Analog-to-digital conversion

A way of changing a continuously variable (**analog**) signal into a stepped (**digital**) signal without loss of information.

Digital signals can be sent more reliably and more efficiently than analog signals. Digital signals can easily be separated from "noise" on the line. Also, **computers** "talk" and "think" in a digital way. ADCs are used in many telephone **modems** because the telephone lines are analog.

Add-on

A piece of **hardware** or **software** that is used to extend the use of the original unit. A sound **card** is an add-on, as is a special filter that "plugs in" to a **graphics program** to change the nature of an **image**. Special software allows an add-on **device** to be recognized by the main **computer**. The term **plug-in** is often used only for software.

Address

The unique electronic whereabouts of a person or business on the **Internet**.

◀ **Adapter**—This adapter is for connecting a monitor to a computer.

In **e-mail** terms it consists of two parts separated by an **@** symbol. The first part identifies the person or department at a **server**, for example, *info@grolier.com* means the information department at *grolier.com*'s server. The second part is the main server address. An Internet address is also known as an **IP address** and can be a set of numbers rather than letters. For example:

123.456.789.01

A **web page** address is also called a **URL** (uniform resource locator), for example:

http://www.grolier.com

ADSL
Asymmetric digital subscriber line

Technology for transmitting **digital** information to homes and businesses using existing phone lines. It is an "always-on" connection. It is much faster than **ISDN** and vastly faster than normal **dial-up** connections.

Most users want to receive more information from the **Web** than they want to send to the Web.

The term asymmetric is used because most connections transmit to the user, and only a few receive information from the user.

AGP

(*See:* **Accelerated graphics port**.)

Alias

A desktop **icon** in **Macintosh operating systems** for a particular **program** or **data** object.

Aliasing

When creating sound and pictures, false (aliasing) frequencies are often produced alongside the correct ones. This produces a jagged edge on **screen text** and adds a buzz to sounds. (*See also:* **Antialiasing**.)

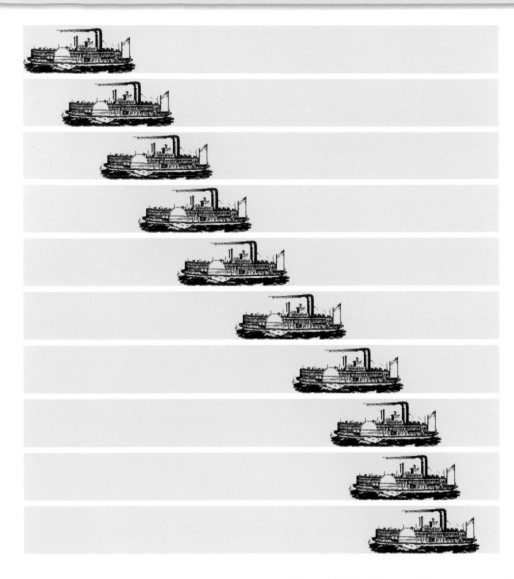

series of connected images that are displayed quickly, one after the other, to give the impression of movement. An animated GIF can loop endlessly (which is what usually happens with advertisements).

Anonymous e-mail
Does not identify the person who sent the message.

Anonymous FTP
Anonymous file transfer protocol
Used to get **access** to a **server** in order to **download files** that are publicly available. When the server asks for a user ID, you simply type "anonymous," and you can use anything for a **password**.

Antialiasing
The smoothing of an **image**, **text**, or sound. Antialiasing is widely used in **computer graphics programs**. (*See also:* **Aliasing**.)

Analog
Signals or information that are carried on a continuously varying wave. It contrasts to **digital** signals, which are discrete steps. (*See also:* **ADC**.)

Anchor
A place of reference for a **hyperlink** in **HTML** (hypertext markup language). If you see a word on a **web page** that is a different color or is underlined, it means the word is an anchor that has a hyperlink to a target somewhere else.

Animated GIF
A moving **graphic image** on a **web page**. Animated **GIFs** are seen on many advertisement **banners**. Each one is made up of a

▲ **Animated GIF**—This series of images or "frames" makes up the parts of an animated GIF. The GIF file displays one image after the other, and the viewer is given the illusion that the image is continuously moving.

In the illustration above, the steamboat can be made to speed up and slow down by varying the distance it moves between frames. In this case the steamboat is slowing down.

▼ **Antialiasing**—The letter below has been smoothed using antialiasing. The image has been enlarged to exaggerate the effect you see on screen.

Antivirus software

Programs that search a **computer's memory devices** (for example, **hard drives**, **Zip drives**, Jazz drives, and floppy disks or **diskettes**) for any known or potential **viruses** (harmful programs). Because so many viruses have been written, any computer that is connected to the **Internet** or other computers, or that shares storage devices with other computers, will need antivirus **software installed**.

New viruses are being created all the time, and so antivirus software needs updating frequently, sometimes as often as once a week.

Most viruses are written to harm people using the **Windows operating system** because it is the most popular operating system, and therefore the virus has the potential to do the most harm. Some viruses appear in **macros**, others in **attachments** to **e-mails**.

Applet

A small **application** that can be sent along with a **web page** to provide animation or perform a calculation, for example. (*See also:* **Active X**.)

AppleTalk

A **LAN** (local area network) that allows **Macintosh computers** to talk with one another and with **devices**, such as **printers**, connected to them.

Appliance

In computers a kind of cheaper **computer** that only performs basic tasks such as connection to the **Internet**.

Application

Short for application program. It is a **program** written to do a particular task, such as act as a **word processor** or display pictures.

Many applications are sold with labels that say **Windows** or **Mac**, since they are the two most commonly used **operating systems**.

Applications work using the **computer's** own operating system and are generally not transferable between operating systems. (*See also:* **Killer App**.)

Archive

A collection of **computer files** that have been **backed up** and taken off the main computer so that the **hard disk** is not clogged up with little-used files.

The entire contents of hard disks are often archived for security reasons, in case the computer crashes, and the active files are damaged beyond repair.

Archiving **programs** can compress files so that they take up less space. The name of a compressed file may end with *.zip* (*see:* **Compression** and **Zip**).

ASCII
American standard code for information interchange

The usual **format** for **text files** in **computers** and on the **Internet**. Every letter, number, or symbol on a **keyboard** is represented by a seven-**bit binary** number (consisting of 0s and 1s). There are 128 possible characters.

@ at, address sign

A symbol used for **e-mail**, pronounced "at." It separates the name of the user from the **Internet address**, for example:

info@grolier.com

It is one of the standard characters on a typewriter and became one of the special standard characters for **computer keyboards**, **programs**, and online message transmission.

Its use goes back to 1972, when Ray Tomlinson, one of the pioneers of e-mail, needed a way to separate the name of the user from the address of a user's machine. He wanted a character that would not be found in the user's name but was on all standard keyboards. He first thought of the punctuation marks and then chose the @ sign because it was distinctive, and because it also meant "at."

Attachment

A **file** sent with an **e-mail**. It might contain pictures, sound, and the like, while the e-mail might contain just **text**. Attachments are not supposed to be very large files. Large files should be transfered by **FTP**. (*See also:* **pdf**.)

Authentication

A way of making sure that only authorized people can get **access** to a **site** or to information. It is commonly used when connecting to an **ISP** through the process of logging on. **Log-on** authentication uses **passwords**.

Autoresponder

A **computer program** that returns a message automatically to anyone who sends **e-mail** to a particular **Internet address**. Autoresponders let someone know that an e-mail has arrived successfully.

If one autoresponder replies to an address that also contains an autoresponder, then both machines can become part of an endless loop that can transfer thousands of useless messages an hour.

B

B2B
Business-to-business

The way business is done among companies via the **Internet**. Often, the **web site** of a business is like a permanent trade show, allowing other businesses to find products and services they may want. When these sites carry business information, they may be **password** protected from all but trading partners. That is different from the way in which businesses try to target consumers over the Internet, which is called **e-tailing**.

B-channel

The part of a signal that carries or bears (hence B) the **data** in an **ISDN** system. The D-channel carries control and signaling information.

Babbage, Charles

The 19th-century English mathematician and inventor who designed a "difference engine" and an "analytical engine." They are considered to be the world's first computing machines. He also founded the British Association for the Advancement of Science and the Royal Astronomical Society. (*See also:* **Computer**.)

Backbone

A main cable that carries **data** fed in from smaller lines (an idea similar to a trunk river and its tributaries).

On the **Internet** a backbone is a main line that carries data between major centers, or **hubs**.

Backup

The process of copying information held on a **hard disk** for security reasons. If a **computer** crashes and **data** is lost, the data from the backup can then be used. If a computer is stolen or destroyed by fire, the fact that data has been backed up and the backup kept at a different location means that precious information still exists.

Most experienced computer operators back up their data frequently, often every hour or so.

Backup can be to a different **storage device** such as a floppy disk (*see:* **Diskette**), a ZIP disk (*see:* **Zip drive**), a JAZZ disk, or a **CD-R**. It can also be to a **server** via an **Internet** connection.

(*See also:* **Archive**.)

Bandwidth

The amount of **data** transfered or received per unit of time. The bigger the bandwidth, the faster the data can be transfered. It is measured in **bits** per second (bps). A **modem** that works at 57,600bps has twice the bandwidth of a modem that works at 28,800bps.

Banner

A strip of (usually) advertising at the top of a **web site**. It is one of the ways in which web site owners try to make money from their **sites**. Many banners use **animated GIFs**.

BASIC
Beginner's all-purpose symbolic instruction code

A simple and very popular **computer** programming language. It was designed by John Kemeney and Thomas Kurtz in 1963.

BASIC can be learned quickly and works with most **operating systems**. Microsoft developed Visual Basic to make BASIC even easier to use on modern computers.

Baud

A term first used to describe the speed at which **data** moved along telegraph wires. It was also applied to **modems** and other **devices** that could send and receive data. It has now been replaced by bps (**bits** per second). Named for Jean-Maurice-Emile Baud, a French engineer.

BBS
Bulletin-board system

A **host computer** that can be reached directly by computer **modem** dialing so that messages can be exchanged directly. To connect to the BBS, you simply need to know the phone number.

There may be over 40,000 BBS in the world, although no one is quite sure because they are informal and not registered anywhere. Most are devoted to special interests, such as bird-watching. They work independently of the **Internet**.

Most recently, some BBS have started **web sites**. Internet **access providers** also have bulletin-board systems that allow Internet users to **download** any necessary **software** to get connected. They are where much online **chat** takes place.

BCC, BC
Blind carbon copy

An **e-mail** feature that allows you to send a copy of your message to someone without the main receiver knowing that you have done so.

When you use the "cc" box, the main receiver sees that the message has been copied to someone else.

Bean

Reusable part of a **Java program**.

BeOS

A personal **computer operating system** designed to be suited especially to **multimedia applications**. It can be used alongside **Windows** or **Mac** operating systems.

Beta test

A second development or testing stage in getting a piece of **software** to work. The software is given to members of the public to try out and report back any **bugs** they find.

Binary

The number system used in **computers** to represent **data**. The binary system has only two numbers: 0 and 1. (*See also:* **Bit**.)

Binary	Decimal
0	0
1	1
10	2
11	3
100	4
101	5
110	6
111	7
1000	8
1001	9
1010	10
etc.	etc.

BinHex

A system designed for converting **Macintosh files** into a form that is easily transported over the **Internet**. It can also be used in **Windows systems**. The file is converted by the sender and has to be reconverted by the receiver. On the desktop these files have names ending in *.hqx*.

BIOS

Basic input/output system

The **program** used by a **PC microprocessor** to start up the **computer**. It is also responsible for managing connections between the computer and **devices** such as the **hard disk** and **printer**.

The BIOS is preinstalled in the computer **hardware**, loaded into an erasable programmable read-only **memory** (EP-ROM) **chip,** and is not part of the **operating system**.

It is the BIOS that **boots** up (starts up) the computer and checks to make sure all the hardware is working. Then it loads the operating system into

the computer's **RAM** (random access memory), from where it is installed on the hard disk. (*See also:* **Motherboard**.)

Bit

Binary digit

The smallest unit of **data** in a **computer**, a bit has a single **binary** value of 0 or 1. Most data is bundled into groups of eight bits called **bytes**. Half a byte (four bits) is called a nibble. Bit is abbreviated with a small "b."

Bit map, bitmap

The location and color of all the pieces of information that make up an **image**, for example, a photograph, on a **computer screen**. The image is displayed in tiny blocks called **pixels**, so the bit map contains information for each pixel. (*See also:* **Computer graphics** and **Raster graphics**.)

Bit rate

The speed at which information is transfered across a **network**. It is measured in kilobits (thousands of **bits**) per second.

Bit stream

A continuous flow of **data**, in **bits**, along a cable or by radio waves.

Board

(*See:* **Circuit board**.)

Boilerplate

A method of writing a **computer program** that makes sure that something happens in all circumstances. The downside is that it usually results in the writing of a rather long-winded and slow piece of **code**.

Bookmark

A **link** to a place on the **Web** that is stored in a list on a **computer**.

Keeping bookmarks allows you to get quickly back to a page without having to type in the **address**.

Bookmarks is the term used by **Netscape**; the same tool in **Internet Explorer** is called Favorites. (*See also:* **Browser**.)

Boot

The starting up of a **computer**. "To boot up a computer" means to start it up and load the **operating system** into the computer's **memory**. A bootable drive is one that contains a copy of the operating system (for example, **Windows**). Reboot is the process of restarting the computer.

Installing puts the operating system onto the **hard drive** for the first time.

When a system is booted, the basic input/output system (**BIOS**) on the computer is "woken up" and does a power-on self-test to make sure everything is in working order. Then it looks at the main hard drive (often drive C on a **PC**) and gets the operating system going.

The operating system then begins to copy information from the **system files**. The first piece is called the Master Boot Record, or Master Boot Block. This record now controls the computer and begins to load the initial system file into the **RAM**, where it will be available very quickly. Then the rest of the system is loaded.

Some peripheral **devices** can sometimes be plugged in while the operating system is still working. This can be referred to as hot-booting the device. If the device can only be connected when the operating system is shut down, it is called cold-booting the device.

Bot

(*See:* **Crawler** and **Spider**.)

Browser

An **application** program that can provide **access** to the **Web** for looking around different locations and pages. **Internet Explorer** and **Netscape** are the most common web browsers.

Web browsers use a special communications system called **HTTP** (hypertext transfer protocol). This **protocol** is shown at the start of a web **address** as http.

The browser allows the **computer** to access a **web site** or **web page** using a web address (**URL**). The browser interacts with the web pages to retrieve and present information and instructions. A browser will also access any page held on the **host** computer, or a **CD**, provided the page is written in the **HTML** (web) language. (*See also:* **Bookmark** and **WAP**.)

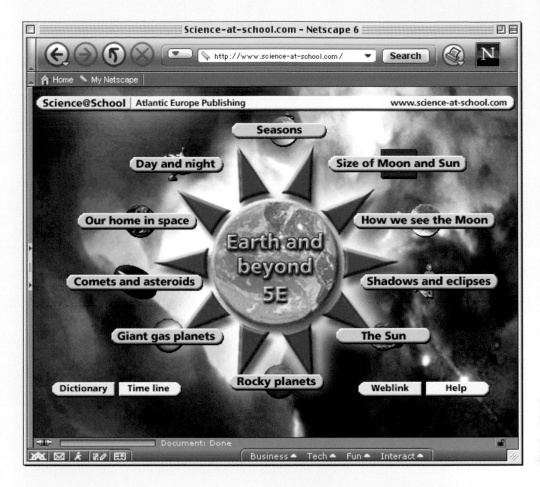

▲ **Browser**—This is how a web site looks using the Netscape 6 browser. Compare it to the Internet Explorer browser. (Other versions of this browser will produce slightly different views.)

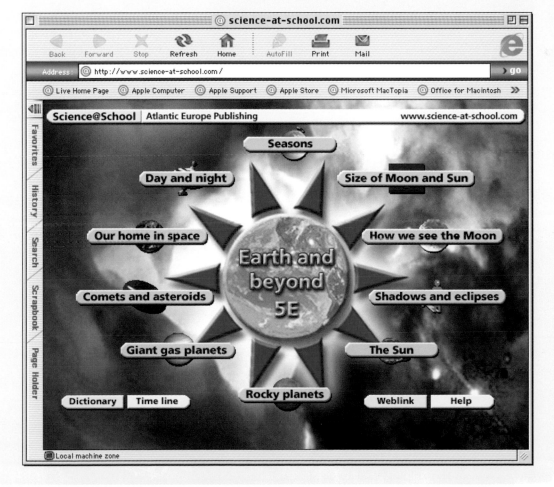

◄ **Browser**—This is how a web site looks with Internet Explorer 5. Compare it to how the same page looks with Netscape. (Other versions of this browser will produce slightly different views.)

Bug

A fault in a **computer program** (an error in the program **code**). Because programs are so complex, it is very difficult to make sure that they work in all possible circumstances. The process of trying to get rid of bugs is called **debugging**. (*See also:* **Patch**.)

It is unlikely that any large program is bug-free.

Burn

Refers to the transfer of information to a **CD-R** or **CD-RW**. The physical indentations on the surface of a CD-R are literally burned, or melted, into the surface using a laser.

Bus

A common pathway connecting many **devices**. Each device on a bus has its own reference number (identity), and only signals sent with the appropriate identity are picked up by the device. All other devices ignore the signals. The term may come from a comparison with buses, which pick up and drop passengers along their routes. (*See also:* **Motherboard** and **USB**.)

Byte

A unit of information that is eight **bits** long and represents a character such as a "g" or an "r" or a "3." A byte may also contain a part of an **image**.

Byte is abbreviated as a large "B." **Computer storage** and **file** sizes are usually measured in bytes. For example, a **hard drive** may have a storage capacity of 9GB (nine **gigabytes**)—nine billion pieces of information.

(*See also:* **Kilobyte**; **Megabyte**; **Terabyte**.)

C

C

A programming language used to construct **operating systems** for **computers**. C++ is a version of the C language that is suitable for creating **image**-based **applications**. **Java** uses a language that is similar to C++.

Cable modem

A **modem** designed to connect a **PC** to a local cable television line. It is an extremely fast connection so long as there are not too many other users logging on at the same time and using the same cable.

Cache

A temporary store for information or a section of high-speed **memory** that stores information recently used by the processor.

Web browsers put recently **surfed web pages** into a special cache in the **computer's memory**. This speeds up **access time** because, if you want to get to that page again, it can be accessed from the **hard drive** instead of the **Internet**.

Cache memory is often called **virtual memory** and is a part of the hard drive used as a kind of **RAM**.

CAD
Computer-aided design

Special **software** used by architects, engineers, and others to create technical illustrations.

Cam

A video camera connected to a **computer**. It is often called a live cam.

Although it is a video camera, it is designed to take still **images** rather than **movies**. A live cam continually updates itself.

Ski resorts and vacation places often keep live cam images on their **web sites** to show the latest conditions.

Card

Short for expansion card. It is a **circuit** designed to increase the capability of the **computer**.

◀ **Card**—A name for any specialized piece of hardware containing processors that give the main computer added functionality. A sound card, which enables the computer to play stereo sound, is a common example of a card. The card shown below is an ethernet card.

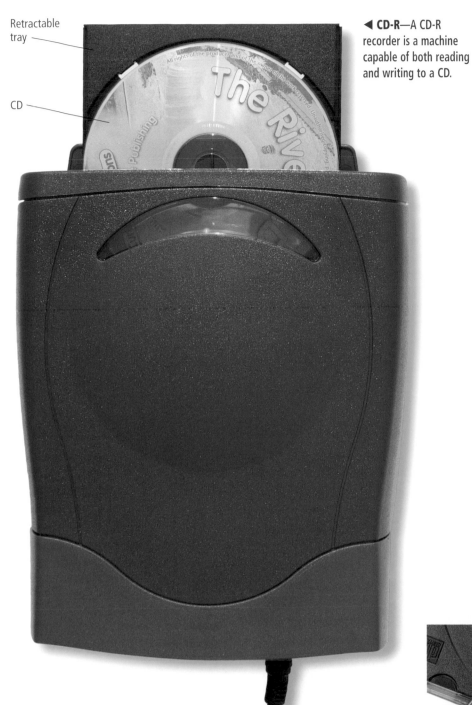

Retractable tray

CD

◀ **CD-R**—A CD-R recorder is a machine capable of both reading and writing to a CD.

CD-Rs can only be written to once. They are often used to **archive** data, for example, the work done during a day in an office.

A CD-R is supplied blank for users to add their own data. (*See also:* **Burn** and **CD-RW**.)

CD-ROM
Compact disk read-only memory or media

A compact disk on which **data** was put by the manufacturer, and which is read using a laser. The laser travels along the disk, following the bumps and pits created during the manufacture, and translates them into **digital** information that the **computer** can handle. CD-ROMs are pressed out from a glass master disk.

CD-RW

A compact disk that can be written onto many times, just like a floppy disk (*see:* **Diskette**). It is supplied blank for users to add their own **data**. (*See also:* **Burn**.)

▼ **CD-ROM**—CD-ROMs typically have a storage capacity of 650MB.

The card is plugged into the **motherboard** of the computer; and the **device** to be driven by the card, for example, loudspeakers or a **monitor**, is connected to a plug on the card.

Cascading style sheet

A new feature of **web pages** that allows the programmer to have much more control over the size and appearance of the **text** and other features.

CD-R
Compact disk-recordable

A compact disk that **data** can be recorded onto using a compact disk writer. It is different from a **CD-ROM**, on which the data for the disk was put by the manufacturer and can only be read, not written.

CGI
Common gateway interface

A standard way for communicating with a **web server**, widely used to help a user fill in forms or get interactive information. The **application** that handles the user's request is kept on the server. It is part of the Web's **HTTP protocol**.

The CGI information and **programs** are kept in a special folder on the server called the CGI bin. An application in this folder (usually written in a programming language called **Perl**) then handles the **data**.

From the server the information can be passed to different types of **operating systems**, allowing **Mac** and **Windows** users, for example, to **access** the information. (*See also:* **Gateway**.)

◄ **Chip**—A chip can be any kind of integrated circuit or microprocessor.

▼**Circuit/circuit board**—The board is the plastic sheet on which copper circuitry and components are placed. This picture shows the underside of a board, on which the connections are made. The central square feature is the underside of a microprocessor.

Channel

A pathway for information. A connection to the **Internet**, for example, may use several pathways. Each of them would be called a channel.

Chassis

The metal framework in which all of the components of the **computer** are housed. The chassis is an internal structure, and you only see it if you take off the computer casing, or outer housing.

Chat

To have a live conversation online. (*See also:* **Abbreviations used in chat**.)

Chip

Short for **microchip**. Also known as **ICs**, or integrated circuits, chips are microprocessors and contain complete **circuits** in miniaturized form. They are at the heart of a **computer**.

A chip is made using a sliver of pure silicon. The circuit and electronic components are etched onto the chip. (*See also:* **Accelerated graphics port; BIOS; RAM; ROM**.)

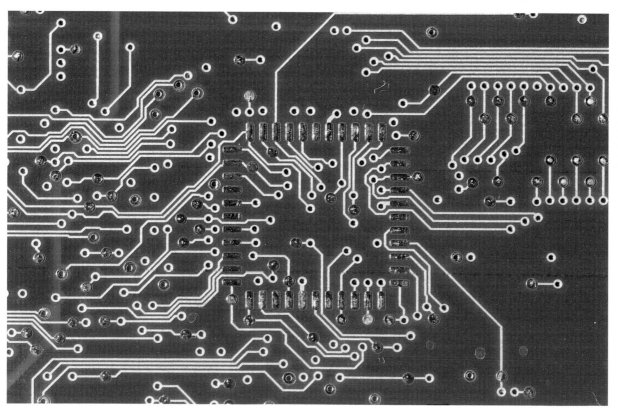

Circuit, circuit board

The sheet of plastic that carries a printed circuit and components. It is also called a circuit board. The main **computer** board is called the **motherboard**. (*See also:* **Chip** and **Microchip, microprocessor**.)

Clip art

Pictures created for general use rather than for a specific job. The illustrations shown here are **freeware** clip art drawings. The rest of the illustrations in this book were all made specifically for it.

Clip art is useful any time you need a simple **image** quickly.

▼▶ **Clip art**—These are typical examples of clip art.

Clock speed

The number of "ticks" or electrical pulses per second that control the speed at which all actions in a **computer** take place.

The computer clock is not like an ordinary clock, but consists of a piece of **circuit** that sends out electrical ticks. When one of these ticks is sent, all the computer's instructions move forward one step.

Computer clocks are usually measured in **MHz**—megahertz, or a million pulses per second (*see:* **Hertz**). Modern computer clocks run at several hundred MHz and have now reached **GHz** (gigahertz, or a billion pulses per second). The clock speed that manufacturers can achieve has been doubling every year. As recently as 1990 computer clocks ran at only 4.77 MHz.

COBOL
Common business-oriented language

A programming language designed for business **applications**, such as figuring out payrolls for staff in a company. COBOL was the first attempt to make a programming language that was similar to ordinary written English.

Code

The **computer** instructions written in a programming language such as **HTML** or **C**. (*See also:* **Boilerplate**; **Bug**; **Debugging**; **Compiler**; **Encryption**; **Source code**.)

com

Used by businesses registering a **web site** (**domain**), such as *grolier.com*.

(*See also:* **Dotcom company**.)

Compiler

A **program** that translates programming **code** into a form that the **computer's** processor can understand.

▼ **Code**—HTML text code for a web site.

```
<!DOCTYPE HTML PUBLIC "-//W3C//DTD HTML 4.01 Frameset//EN"
    "http://www.w3.org/TR/1999/REC-html401-19991224/frameset.dtd">
<html>

<head>

<title>Science-encyclopedia</title>

</head>

<frameset cols="130,510,*" frameborder="0" border="NO" framespacing="0" marginwidth="0" marginheight="0">

<frame name="LeftBar" src= "contents.html" scrolling="no" frameborder="no" border="0" border="no"
    framespacing="0" marginwidth="0" marginheight="0">

<frame name="displayPanel" src="readText.html"
    scrolling="auto" frameborder="no" border="0" border="no" framespacing="0"
    marginwidth="0" marginheight="0">

<frame name="bleedRight" src="../MastheadRight.html"
    scrolling="no" frameborder="no" border="0" border="no" framespacing="0"
    marginwidth="0" marginheight="0">
</frameset>

</html>
```

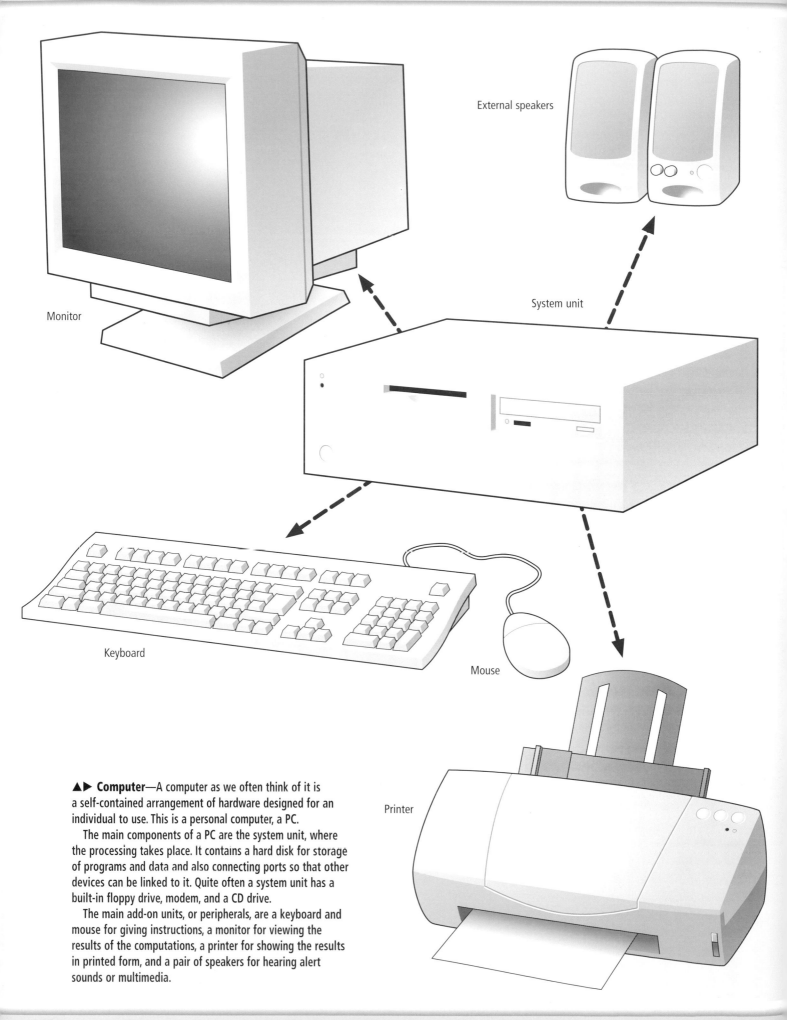

External speakers

System unit

Monitor

Keyboard

Mouse

Printer

▲▶ **Computer**—A computer as we often think of it is
a self-contained arrangement of hardware designed for an
individual to use. This is a personal computer, a PC.

The main components of a PC are the system unit, where
the processing takes place. It contains a hard disk for storage
of programs and data and also connecting ports so that other
devices can be linked to it. Quite often a system unit has a
built-in floppy drive, modem, and a CD drive.

The main add-on units, or peripherals, are a keyboard and
mouse for giving instructions, a monitor for viewing the
results of the computations, a printer for showing the results
in printed form, and a pair of speakers for hearing alert
sounds or multimedia.

Compression, compressing

A way of making **data** smaller and thus faster and cheaper to send between **computers** or over the **Internet**. The long string of **bits** used in many **word processors** to indicate a space can be replaced with a piece of **code** that uses fewer bits. A small number of bits can also be used to represent a character that is normally eight bits long. In this way **text files** can be compressed to half their original size.

When they are received, some compressed files have to be uncompressed. Names that include "zip" are common compressed **formats** (*see:* **Zip**).

Images can also be compressed using file formats such as **JPEG**, **GIF**, and **PNG**.

(*See also:* **Acrobat**; **pdf**; **Portable device/document**.)

Computer

A machine that uses **digital** information and a set of instructions called a **program** (or **application**) to produce a result.

A computer will normally have a place for storing **data** (a **hard drive**), programs, and various connectors (called **ports**) for receiving and sending out data.

Originally, a computer was the name given to a person, a clerk, whose job it was to add up sets of numbers. The first nonhuman computer was a machine invented by Charles **Babbage** in the 19th century. He called it an "analytical engine." Babbage's assistant, Ada Lovelace, invented the idea of a program to supply instructions. She is therefore thought of as the world's first programmer.

Babbage could not produce a computer in the mechanical age. That had to wait until the invention

Computer graphics

Any **images** produced on, or manipulated, by a **computer**. Powerful **software** allows either paintinglike or technical drawing-like images to be produced.

Computer graphics can be produced either with **keyboard** commands, by using a **mouse**, or with a pressure sensitive **tablet** and a penlike object that presses on the tablet (called a stylus). Images such as photographs and hand-drawn or painted artwork can also be brought into the computer by using a **scanner**.

Computer graphics (also called digital artwork) are now widely used instead of traditional, hand-painted or drawn artwork.

(*See also:* **Animated GIF**; **Antialiasing**; **Bit map**; **CAD**; **Clip art**; **Graphic**; **Raster graphics**; **Vector graphics**.)

of such devices as vacuum tubes, transistors, and integrated circuits. These changes made the computer a cheaper, more flexible device that could be used in every home.

Electronic computers were developed during World War II. They were first created in Great Britain and then in the United States, where development was faster. Early pioneers at this time included John **von Neumann**, who thought up the idea of the stored program.

(*For types of computer see:* **Desktop**; **Laptop**; **Mac, Macintosh**; **Mainframe**; **Palmtop**; **PC**; **Server**; **Supercomputer**; **Terminal**; **Tower**.)

(*For computer components see:* **Accelerated graphic port**; **BIOS**; **Card**; **Chassis**; **Chip**; **Circuit**; **Clock speed**; **CPU**; **Graphical user interface**; **IC**; **Microchip**; **Motherboard**; **RAM**; **ROM**; **System unit**.)

(*For graphic formats see:* **GIF**; **JPEG**; **TIFF**; and pages 22 to 23.)

Configuration

(*See:* **Initialization**.)

Cookie

A small package of information that a **web site** puts onto the user's **hard disk**. For example, it might contain **preferences** or a **password** for **access** to a site, or it might store information about which **banner** advertisement was last displayed to make sure the next one is different.

The information in the cookie can be examined by the web **server** at a later date. It is possible to view the cookies that have been stored on your **hard disk** (although the information may be in **code**). **Internet Explorer** stores cookies as separate **files** under a **Windows** subdirectory. **Netscape** stores cookies in a single cookies *.txt* file.

Counter

A **program** that counts the number of people who have visited a page on a **web site**. (*See also:* **Hit**.)

CPU

Central processing unit
The main **microprocessor** on a **computer motherboard**.

Crawler

A **program** designed to visit **web sites**, read the pages, and then compile a list of them for a **search engine**. Crawlers are also known as **spiders** and bots.

Crossover cable

A wire that is used to connect two computers by "crossing over," or reversing, their connections. It saves the cost of a **hub** (which does the same job, but for a number of devices or computers).

Cursor

The small I-bar, pointer, or other shape used to show the active position on a **computer monitor**. By changing its shape, a cursor can also indicate other things, such as waiting.

Cyber-

A prefix used to describe something connected to the **computer** age. *Kybernetes* is the Greek word for "steersman" that gave rise to the word cybernetics, the science of communication and control (including robotics).

Cyberpunk and **cyberspace** are just two of many newly coined "cyber" words.

Cyberspace

The total environment of all the interconnected **computers** in the world.

D

DAT
Digital audio tape

A standard way of recording audio or **data** for professional use. It is effectively a high-quality **digital** tape recorder. Its main uses include storing the material needed to create a **CD-R** master and **archiving** large amounts of data.

Data

In **computers** information in numerical form that can be **digitally** transmitted or processed.

Database

A collection of **data** arranged so that the contents are easy to **access**. A list of names and addresses held on a **computer** is one type of simple database. (*See also:* **SQL**.)

Debugging

The process of removing **bugs** (errors) in programming **code**. A **program** containing many bugs is called "buggy."

Special programs have been written to help find some of the more predictable bugs. They are called debugging tools.

Default

The set of values that the **computer** will use if it receives no **preferences** from the user. For example, **word processors** default to a standard size and type of **font**.

Defragmenter

A **program** that reorganizes the **files** on a **computer's hard drive** so that all the sections belonging to one piece of **data** follow one another in close sequence.

A hard drive becomes fragmented after a while because the computer fills empty spaces on it no matter where they occur. Thus you may write a piece of information to a hard disk and then, sometime later, delete that information. The computer then sees this space as an empty slot in which to put new information, no matter what its size. If the information is too big for the slot, the computer fills the slot, puts marks at the end of the data, and puts the rest of the data in the next available slot. As a result, what was once a single piece of data is fragmented into two segments or more. That is very efficient for using the space on the drive,

but it slows down the speed at which the computer can read the data. Defragmenting is an important routine job, and it is often recommended that drives be defragmented about once a month. Special **programs** are sold to do it.

Desktop

The starting **screen** shown when the **computer operating system** has finished **booting**. It is a kind of "home-base."

It was developed to aid people who were new to computing and who needed to think of their computer screen as an imaginary desktop on which all the **files** and folders were laid out. They would then be able to use a **mouse** to pick up and move the files and folders around in this **virtual** world. Anything to do with the desktop is given the prefix desktop. So, for example, "desktop files" means the files visible on the desktop.

Desktop computer

A type of personal **computer** that is small enough to fit conveniently on a desktop. Compare it to a **laptop**, **palmtop**, or **mainframe** computer.

Many desktop computers have the **system unit** arranged so that it sits underneath the **monitor**. More powerful system units, and especially those that need additional **cards**, cannot use this configuration and tend to be built into **towers**.

▶ **Desktop computer**—Office desktop computers have usually had separately replaceable system units and monitors (left). Integrated desktop computers have recently been introduced, of which the i-Mac is an example, that provide a more compact use of space (far right). They have been adopted widely in homes where people want to match the computer to the decor of the room.

Device

Any piece of **computer hardware**. It might mean an external **hard drive**, a **modem**, a **keyboard**, and so on. A device is replaceable, so it does not include the computer **motherboard**, but it does include the hard drive inside the computer case.

DHTML
Dynamic HTML

A form of **HTML** that is suited for the design of more active **web pages** that have animations, interactive parts, special typeface styles, and so on.

Dial-up

The process of connecting to the **Internet** by using a **modem** that dials a telephone number to connect the user to an **ISP** (Internet service provider). (*See also:* **ADSL** and **ISDN**.)

Digital

Anything electronic that works with a system that has only two states: on or off. They are

▲▶ **Diskette**—This is the original form of removable storage, or media. It typically can hold up to 1.44MB of data. It is still used but rapidly being replaced by larger storage devices like Zip cartridges.

expressed in digital **data** by the numbers 1 and 0.

In **computers** digital information is stored as a series of 1s and 0s. Each of these digits is called a **bit**; a packet of eight bits (which are typically needed to describe a character like "a" or "b") is called a **byte**. (*See also:* **ACD**; **Analog**; **Binary**.)

DIMM
Dual inline memory module

A form of **memory chip** that is equivalent to a double **SIMM**. That means it can support twice the **data** transfer of a SIMM.

Directory

A way of organizing information. Computers contain groups of related **files**. Each of them contains a directory, or an organized list of its contents. (*See also:* **Root directory**.)

Disk

(*See:* **Diskette** and **Hard disk**.)

Diskette

A small, **portable device** that stores **data** in the form of magnetic media. It is also called a floppy, or floppy disk.

The original diskettes were 5.25 inches across, but they were replaced by 3.5 inch diskettes that can hold about 1.44 **megabytes** of information.

For many purposes these diskettes are too small and slow for modern use, and they are now being replaced by **Zip drives** and other drives that have disks that can hold 100MB or more of data. (*See also:* **CD-R**; **CD-RW**; **DAT**.)

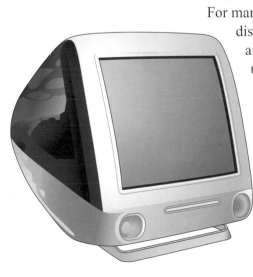

Display, display screen

The visual result of the **computer**, shown on a **screen** or a **monitor**.

The display is created on the wide end of a cathode-ray tube. An electron beam sweeps across the screen many times a second (often 70 or more). The inside of the screen is coated with tiny dots of material, called phosphors, that glow when struck by the beam. As the beam energizes patterns of phosphors, they glow, their brightness and hue depending on the intensity of the energy they receive. They quickly lose their energy again, however, and so they have to be refreshed by the beam as it travels back and forth across the screen. (*See also:* **Active matrix display**; **LCD, LCD display**; **SVGA**.)

DNS
Domain-name system

The way in which **Internet domain** names in words are translated into the **IP addresses** (Internet protocol addresses) in numbers that can be found by the **computer**.

For example, the domain name abcdef.com might have an IP address of *123.456.789.01*. Because the numbers are hard to remember, the names are used for convenience.

Document

A piece of information, for example, a finished letter from a **word processor**, that is then saved as a **file**. The file is the document.

Domain, domain name

A place on the **Web** identified by a name.

A domain name is the part of the **URL** (uniform resource locator) that tells a **server** where to look for a **web page**.

Every site on the **Internet** must have a unique **address**. To do this efficiently, a string of numbers must be given to each address and it alone. However, since long strings of numbers are not easy to

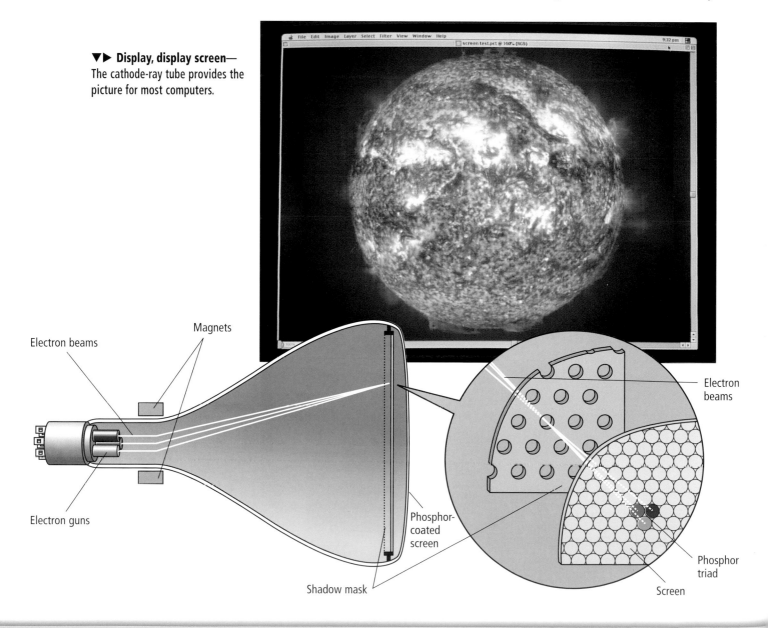

▼▶ Display, display screen—
The cathode-ray tube provides the picture for most computers.

Electron beams

Magnets

Electron guns

Phosphor-coated screen

Shadow mask

Electron beams

Phosphor triad

Screen

remember, word names are used as "handles" for people to type. These word addresses are translated into the necessary numbers inside the user's **computer**. That is why, when you first set up your **browser** or **e-mail program**, you are asked for some strings of numbers as well as your name. These number strings are your Internet service provider's (**ISP**) address on the Internet. (*See also:* **DNS**.)

There are several parts to a domain name. Each part is separated by a period. For example, *www.grolier.com* is made of three parts. The "*www.*" refers to a particular type of communicating system, in this case the World Wide Web. The next part, "*grolier,*" states a specific name, in this case a company. The final part, "*.com,*" indicates that Grolier is a business, which could be a company or an individual.

Domain names registered in the United States are unique in that there is no reference to the country in which they are located. Most other places include an abbreviation of their country as part of their domain name, for example, ending in *.uk* for the United Kingdom, *.de* for Germany (Deutschland), and *.au* for Australia. Noncommercial, United States-registered domain names end in letters such as *.org* (for nonprofit organizations), *.gov* (for government departments), and *.edu* (for academic institutions). Network service providers end in *.net.* Endings in other countries vary. For example, in the UK university domain names end in *.ac* and schools in *.sch*

DOS
Disk-operating system
The first **operating system installed** on **PCs** was developed

for IBM by Bill Gates and his new Microsoft Corporation. He retained the rights to market a Microsoft version, called MS-DOS.

DOS does not have a **graphical user interface** (you have to write all your instructions in words), and so it has largely been replaced by other systems such as **Windows** and **Mac** OS.

The earliest Windows OS was simply an **application** designed to provide a graphic interface that translated user-friendly commands into DOS.

Dot-matrix printer
A **printer** that creates an **image** from a pattern of dots. The first dot–matrix printers were also impact printers, stamping out their image of dots line by line through an inked ribbon in much the same way as a typewriter. Later, the dots became finer, and printers were developed that did not use direct impact, but fine jets of ink or a laser beam.

The finer the dots on the page (known as the higher the resolution), the less the dots can be seen, and the sharper the image. A resolution of 600 dots per inch is now common, producing a very sharp image.

Dotcom company
A **web site** set up for retail sales. The term is used to describe companies that have started up recently in an attempt to make money from the **Internet**. Very few have made a profit.

Download
The process of moving a **file** from a remote **server** where the file is held to one's own **computer**.

People commonly download files from the **Internet** for use on their own computer. When

receiving **e-mails**, you also are actually downloading the files from your own private mailbag on the server of your Internet Service Provider (**ISP**).

For people wanting to transfer many files or large files between computers, the file transfer protocol (**FTP**) is used instead of the "www" **protocol**. When downloading through a **web page**, the FTP request is set up automatically by the web page, so these letters are rarely seen in an **address**. People wanting to send, or **upload**, files to their web pages on a **server** have to use a special (FTP) **application**.

DRAM
Dynamic random access memory
The common type of **RAM** (random access memory) used in **PCs**.

Any kind of quickly accessed **memory** is a **chip** on which there is a network of electrically charged points used to represent 1s and 0s. The **computer** can **access** information held in this way much faster than from a **hard drive**.

Driver
A small **program** that connects a **device** with programs. **Printers** are often connected to **word processors** by drivers. Drivers are often marked as *.dll* files. The driver contains special information about the way the device works.

DVD
Digital versatile disk
An optically read disk that can hold 4.7 **gigabytes** of **data** on each of its two sides. Thus each side can contain enough data to play a full-length movie. This contrasts with **CD-Rs** and **CD-ROMs**, which can only hold 650 **megabytes**.

E

e-

What follows these two characters always has something to do with the **Internet**. It began with **e-mail**, short for electronic mail, but has since been used more widely, for example, e-tailing, meaning retailing over the Internet.

e-book

A portable electronic "book." It is similar in size to a paperback and uses a high-quality **LCD display** and a long-life battery (rechargeable and with a life of 20 hours or so). e-books can hold the equivalent of many paper books (which have now been called treeware).

e-business, e-commerce

A business that works entirely over the **Internet** is called an e-business. Booksellers and **computer** equipment sellers are two of the most noticeable e-businesses on the Net. They rely on special **encryption programs** to protect the information, such as credit card numbers, sent over the Internet.

The activity of buying and selling on the Internet, especially when it is done on a large scale, is called e-commerce. A retailer that is an e-business is called an e-tailer. (*Compare with:* **B2B**.)

e-mail
Electronic mail

A system for sending messages over the **Internet** (or in the case of large companies between departments by **intranet**).

e-mail was one of the first ways in which the Internet was used and is still its most popular **application**. Although e-mail is a very primitive writing tool, by using **attachments**, pictures and other types of files can be sent at the same time as text.

e-mail has the advantage of being both very fast and very cheap. It also allows messages to be sent to many recipients at the same time.

e-mail is one of the **protocols** included with the **TCP/IP** (transport control protocol/Internet protocol) suite (others include "www" and **FTP**). e-mail is often sent using the protocol called **SMTP** (simple mail transfer protocol) and received using the protocol called **POP3**.

(*See also:* **Address**; **Anonymous e-mail**; **@ at, address sign**; **Autoresponder**; **BCC**; **Junk e-mail, spam**; **MIME**; **Snail mail**.)

e-tailing

(*See:* **e-**; **e-business, e-commerce**.)

EDO RAM
Extended data output RAM

A type of **RAM** (random access memory) **chip** that is designed to make it faster to read **data** from memory. It is particularly useful with faster **microprocessors**.

Encryption

The conversion of **data** into a **code** that cannot be read by an unauthorized person such as a **hacker**. It is used to protect financial and other sensitive data sent over the **Internet**.

End user

The person who will finally make use of a **software** or **hardware** product; in effect, the customer.

Ethernet

A system for connecting **computers** within a building to create a **LAN** (local area network).

An ethernet system uses simple (coaxial) cable or pairs of twisted wires.

10 BASE-T is the most commonly used system. It allows **data** to be sent along the ethernet at 10Mbps (megabits per second). Faster ethernet is 100 BASE-T, which works at 100Mbps. (*See also:* **Port** and **RJ**.)

Explorer

(*See:* **Internet Explorer**.)

Extension

1. A **file** containing programming that extends the capabilities of a more basic **program**.
2. A suffix given to identify a file type, for example, *.pdf*, meaning "portable document format" (**pdf**). The suffix *.exe* means the **software** that executes (carries out) a program.

F

FAQ
Frequently asked questions

A list of common queries that people ask a **web site**. FAQ sections on web sites allow answers to be summarized once rather than being sent individually to every person who asks. Most people go to the FAQ section with their problems or questions before asking for individual help.

Favorite

(*See:* **Bookmark**.)

File

A collection of **data**, **programs**, and so on stored in a **computer's memory** or on a **storage device** under a single identifying name called a file name. (*See also:* **Directory** and **Document**.)

File sharing

A system of sharing **computer data** and space on a **LAN** (local area network).

Typically, one member of a LAN will make one or more of their data folders a shared folder. Other members of the **network** can then copy from or send data to this shared file.

Firewall

A set of related **programs** designed to protect a private **network** from the outside world. These programs work at the **gateway** to the protected network, filtering all requests for **data**.

In large networks a firewall is installed on a gateway **computer**, which is isolated from the network. The only way through a firewall is by using a set of **passwords**.

FireWire

A very fast method of connecting external **devices** to a personal **computer** developed by Apple Computer. It allows **data** to be transfered at hundreds of megabits per second. (*See also:* **Port**.)

Floppy disk

(*See:* **Diskette**.)

Font

The particular design of type—for example, Helvetica and Times.

Fonts were first developed for paper printing. The earliest fonts were cast from metal or cut from wood blocks.

Electronic versions of these fonts were produced when **computers** were developed. However, computers allowed fonts to be easily changed, made larger or smaller as a designer pleased. This made computer fonts much more flexible than traditional fonts.

Today, anyone with a personal computer can use it to design pages with any font they choose (there are thousands now available) or even design fonts themselves.

Special fonts have now been designed that are easier to read on a computer **screen**. They include Verdana and Charcoal.

Two types of fonts are available for **printers** and **screen display**. The fonts that come with the computer are called bit-map fonts. They are **digital** representations of fonts whose size cannot be changed. They produce jagged edges and odd-looking shapes for sizes of type that do not match the sizes in the memory. Outline fonts, on the other hand, are mathematical descriptions of the letter forms sent to the printer. They are resized before they get to the printer. The printer only converts them at the last minute to the dots that are printed on the paper. As a result, the printer does not have to try to resize one of its stored fonts, and the font comes out with sharp edges. TrueType and Type 1 fonts are outline fonts and are used with **Postscript** and **PCL** printer languages. (*See also:* **Aliasing** and **Antialiasing**.)

Foo

A **computer** developer's term for "something." It has no meaning of its own and is used while developers are at the planning stage. Later, they will replace "foo" with real pieces of **code**.

For example, a programmer might write:

if (foo) then foo
else
foo

Footprint

The amount of space a piece of **hardware** takes up on a desktop or floor.

Format

A term used in many contexts for the arrangement of information.

1. The type of **data file**, for example, EPS, **TIFF**, **JPEG**, **GIF** (*see pages 22 to 23*.) (*See also:* **MPEG** and **RTF**.)
2. The layout of a page in a book is its format. The same idea is used in page makeup, **word-processing**, and many other **programs**. The purpose of a format is to make the pages orderly and pleasing to look at for the reader.
3. The pattern of organization of data on a drive. A drive is formated by the **operating system** so that all the places on it have a known location. This makes it possible for the drive to be read. **Hard drives** are often formated into areas called sectors, tracks, and clusters.

FORTRAN
FORmula TRANslation

A programming language that was designed for use by engineers and scientists. It has been replaced by the language **C**.

Frames

A method of creating a **web page** with multiple sections that can work independently. A master, or index file, controls each of the frames, but the content of the frames themselves is controlled by **HTML code** written for each frame.

Frames were introduced at a later stage in the development of **Netscape** and **Internet Explorer browsers** and were not supported by earlier browsers.

Frames are very good for helping with **navigation**. There are many examples of the use of frames on the **Web**. One example can be found at: *www.curriculumvisions.com*.

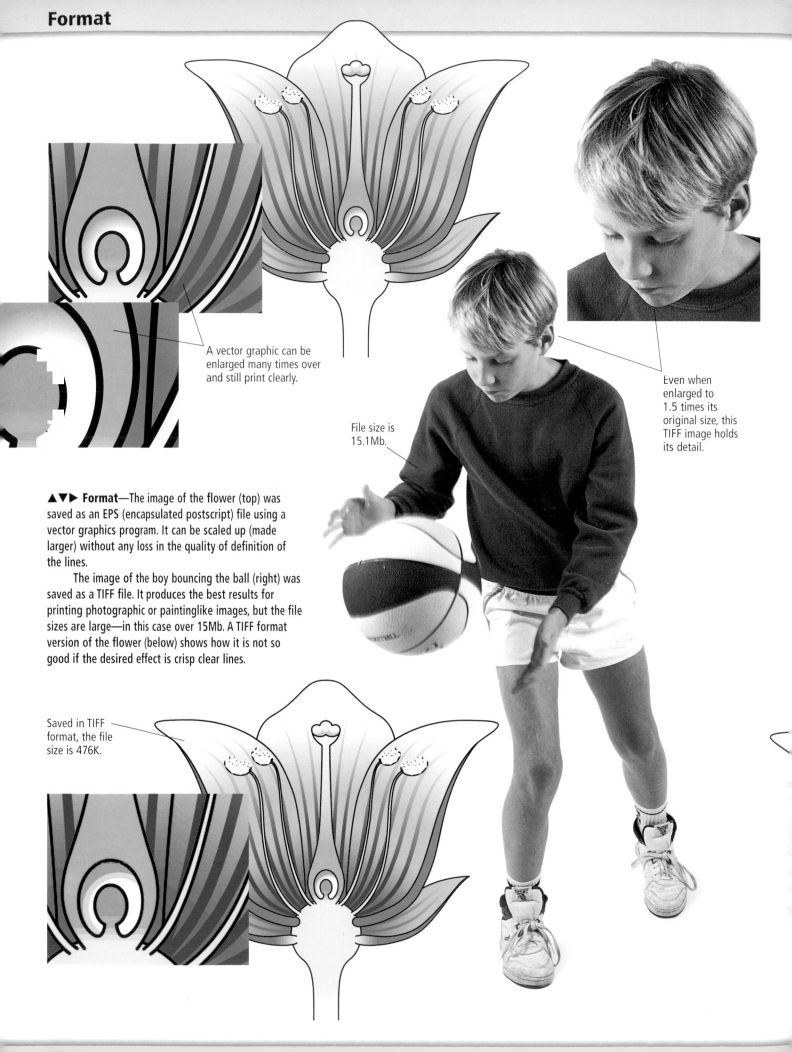

A vector graphic can be enlarged many times over and still print clearly.

Even when enlarged to 1.5 times its original size, this TIFF image holds its detail.

File size is 15.1Mb.

▲▼▶ **Format**—The image of the flower (top) was saved as an EPS (encapsulated postscript) file using a vector graphics program. It can be scaled up (made larger) without any loss in the quality of definition of the lines.

The image of the boy bouncing the ball (right) was saved as a TIFF file. It produces the best results for printing photographic or paintinglike images, but the file sizes are large—in this case over 15Mb. A TIFF format version of the flower (below) shows how it is not so good if the desired effect is crisp clear lines.

Saved in TIFF format, the file size is 476K.

A
(JPEG maximum =
least compression)

File size
is 1.3Mb.

▼ **Format**—Saving an image in JPEG format can make it a lot smaller. Smaller file sizes mean that a file takes up less memory and make for faster downloads on the Web. However, as a file is increasingly compressed, more information is lost, and the quality of the image starts to deteriorate. What degree of compression to use depends on the use, the limitations of the technology, and the user.

B
(JPEG medium =
medium compression)

File size
is 412K.

When enlarged
1.5 times its
original size, this
highly compressed
JPEG starts to show
a deteriorating
image quality.

C
(JPEG minimum =
maximum compression)

File size
is 188K.

▼ **Format**—Although JPEG images are best for photographic or paintinglike images, saving an image as a GIF is often better for images with a lot of contrast, such as text or this picture of the flower. GIFs make file sizes small and are also good for animations (animated GIFs).

JPEG file size
is 124K.

This image of the flower
has been compressed to
its minimum size.

A closeup from a version saved as
a GIF shows how the details on the
lines are better than a JPEG. PNG is
expected to replace the GIF format.

GIF file size
is 128K.

Freeware

Programs (**software**) that are available for others to use without payment. Freeware **sites** exist on the **Internet**. Many freeware programs are also available on the **CD-ROMs** included with computer magazines. The main **browsers**, **Netscape** Communicator and Microsoft **Internet Explorer**, are both freeware.

FTP
File-transfer protocol

A system for sharing **files** over the **Internet**. **Access** is gained to files shared on an FTP **server** site. Many FTP sites are open to everyone. The user simply has to type "anonymous" into the **password** box to download these shared files (*see:* **Anonymous FTP**).

Web site developers use FTP to **upload** web files to a web server. (*See also:* **Download**.)

G

Gateway

A place on a **network** that acts as an entrance to another network. An **ISP** (Internet service provider) is a gateway to the **Internet**. (*See also:* **CGI**.)

Geek (technofreak)

A person so fascinated with technology and terminology that he/she spends an abnormal amount of time on it and sacrifices other things that most people do in their daily lives.

Computer hackers could be said to be geeks with high levels of programming skills. A geek used to be the name for a circus freak in a side show.

(*See also:* **Nerd**.)

GHz
Gigahertz

A billion cycles per second. Used to describe the **clock speed** of very fast **computers**. (*See also:* **Hertz**.)

GIF
Graphics interchange format

Pronounced JIF, it is (along with **JPEG**) one of the most common file **formats** for **graphic images** on the **Web**. A way of **compressing** the image so that it can be transfered quickly over the **Internet**, it is most suitable for diagrams that only need a limited number of colors. Not a suitable format for photographs, it is being replaced by the **PNG** format. (*See also:* **Animated GIF**.)

(*For examples of GIF format see page 23*.)

Gigabyte (GB or Gb)

A unit of **memory** size or **data** equivalent to one billion **bytes**. (*See also:* **Kilobyte**; **Megabyte**; **Terabyte**.)

Gopher

An **Internet application protocol** that was an early version of the one used for the **Web**. It is no longer widely used.

Graphic

In computing, any illustrative material. Most information sources have two kinds of information: one designed to be read as **text**, and one designed to be seen as a drawn illustration or photograph. All kinds of illustration are referred to as graphics. Graphics take up far more **memory** and processing power than text, and handling them therefore dramatically slows down a **computer**.

(*See also:* **Animated GIF**; **Computer graphics**; **Image**; **Raster graphics**; **Vector graphics**.)

Graphical user interface, GUI

A visual way of interacting with a **computer** using **icons**, menus, and windows instead of just words or **code**. It makes the computer more user-friendly, and so a GUI is now used by most modern **operating systems**.

H

Hacker

A person who tries to break into other people's **programs**, often just for the sake of the challenge. Hackers are very good programmers, but hacking is against the law. A person who tries to hack for intentional criminal or malicious reasons is often called a cracker (criminal hacker).

Handshaking

The process of two **modems** "talking." It is often heard as a sequence of rapid beeps. When a modem dials another modem, the sending and receiving modems have to agree what system (**protocol**) to talk in and what speed of communication to use.

Hard drive, hard disk

The main disk on which the **computer** stores information. It is designed to be as fast as possible so that **accessing** the **data** does not keep the **microprocessor** waiting too long. Modern hard drives usually have a capacity of several **gigabytes**.

A hard drive records information in a series of blocks. The disk has a magnetic surface on which the data is held as patterns of magnetic blips. The drive reads from and writes to the disk using a "head," which is an electromagnet. Disk **access time** is measured in milliseconds (thousandths of a second).

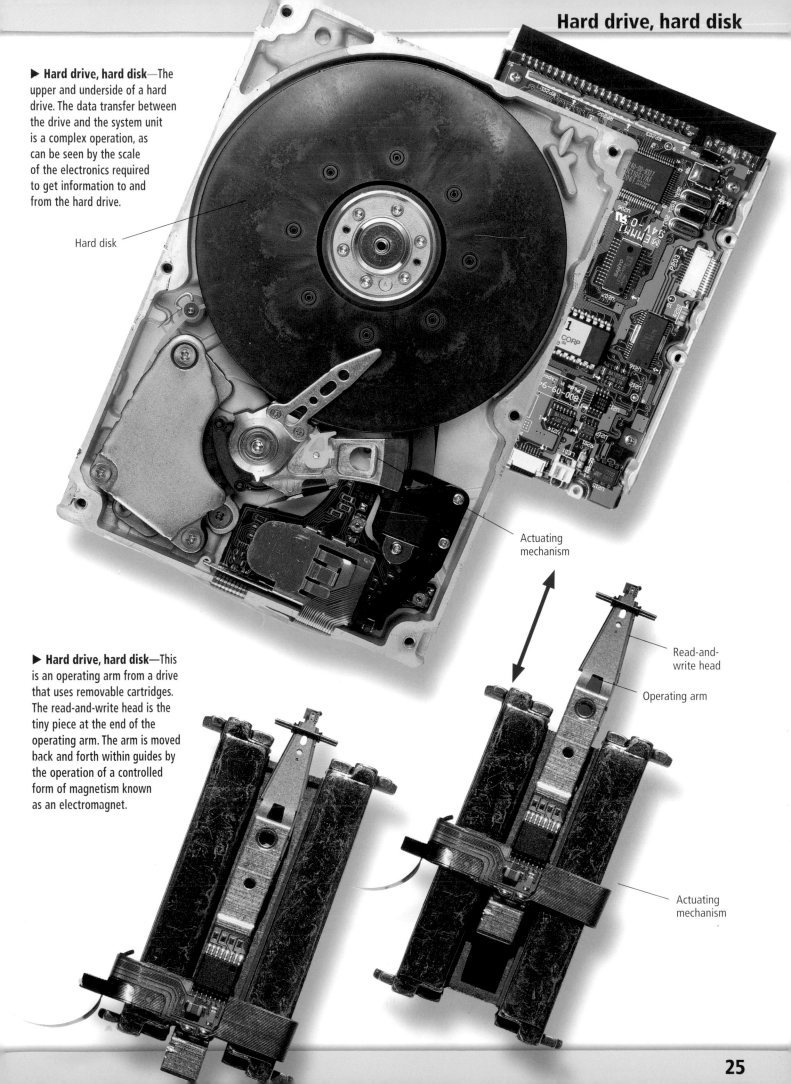

▶ **Hard drive, hard disk**—The upper and underside of a hard drive. The data transfer between the drive and the system unit is a complex operation, as can be seen by the scale of the electronics required to get information to and from the hard drive.

Hard disk

Actuating mechanism

Read-and-write head

Operating arm

▶ **Hard drive, hard disk**—This is an operating arm from a drive that uses removable cartridges. The read-and-write head is the tiny piece at the end of the operating arm. The arm is moved back and forth within guides by the operation of a controlled form of magnetism known as an electromagnet.

Actuating mechanism

Hardware

The physical pieces of a **computer** system, such as the **monitor**, the **system unit**, and **keyboard**. Contrast to **software**, which is a term for the **code** written to make the hardware do specific tasks. (*See also:* **Platform**.)

(*For other hardware see:* **Accelerated graphics port**; **Adapter**; **Add-on**; **Card**; **Chip**; **Circuit**; **CPU**; **Device**; **Hard drive**; **Hub**; **IC**; **Microchip**; **Modem**; **Motherboard**; **Mouse**; **Portable device**; **Printer**; **Scanner**; **Screen**; **Speakers**; **Storage device**; **Tablet**; **Trackball**; **USB**.)

Hertz (Hz)

A unit of frequency, equal to one cycle per second.

It is equal to the number of crests on a wave that pass a fixed point each second. The number of hertz is therefore equal to the number of complete wave cycles per second.

The larger the number of hertz, the higher the sound; in light, the closer the colors are to the red end of the spectrum.

The hertz is named for the 19th-century German physicist Heinrich Hertz.

(*See also:* **Gigahertz**.)

Hit

A request by a user for a page on a **web site**. Counting hits gives the web site owner an idea of the popularity of the site. (*See also:* **Counter**.)

Home page

The **web page** that a **browser** **displays** when first starting up. Browsers are preset with home pages (usually their company's own home page), but they can be reset to another page, for example, to a **search engine** or a news page.

For a **web site** developer a home page is the first page displayed when the web site is requested by a user.

Host

Any **computer** that is connected permanently to the **Internet** and can send and receive information to and from other computers.

HTML
Hypertext markup language

The fundamental programming **code** that is used to display pages on the **Web**. The code, or markup, tells the web **browser** how to display the contents of a **web page**. (*For an example of HTML code see page 13.*)

(*See also:* **Active server page**; **Anchor**; **DHTML**; **Meta**; **Source code**; **Webmaster**; **Web site**; **XHTML**.)

HTTP
Hypertext transfer protocol

The set of rules for exchanging **files** of any kind (text, **images**, sound, and so on) on the **Web**. (*See also:* **CGI**.)

Hub

In computing a place where **data** is exchanged. Hubs are used to interconnect a number of **computers** or peripheral **devices**, such as **printers** and **scanners**, so that they can exchange information. (*See also:* **Backbone** and **Crossover cable**.)

Hyperlink

A **link** on a **web page** that connects a user with some other place on the World Wide Web.

Originally, hyperlinks were simply underlined text, but now buttons, **images**, and even **movies** can act as hyperlinks. (*See also:* **Anchor**.)

I

I/O
Input/output

A **device** or **program** that transfers **data** to and from a **computer**. A **keyboard** is an input-only device; a **modem** is both an input and an output device.

IC
Integrated circuit

Also known as a **chip**, it is a miniature electronic device that can be set up to perform many functions. The most complex chips act as **microprocessors**, but a **computer** uses more than the microprocessor chip for a variety of specialized functions, such as **memory**, **storage**, and **clock**.

Icon

A small **image** that can be clicked to launch a **program** or to open a folder or a **file**. Icons can be used for individual **data** files or for **applications**. (*See also:* **Graphical user interface**.)

▶▼ **Icon**—Examples of desktop icons.

Image

A picture or a diagram. Images can be scanned into the **computer** (*see:* **Scanner**) or can be made electronically, **pixel** by pixel. That is called a **bit map**. Diagrams and other artwork generated in drawing-based **programs** can be stored as instructions so that they can be resized without loss of quality. They are called **vector graphics**. (*See also:* **Clip art**; **Computer graphics**; **Graphic**; **Raster graphics**; **Screen capture**.)

Initialization

To get a **program** going with its starting values as defined by the programmer and possibly modified by the user as **preferences**. It is also known as configuration. (Initialization files are marked *.ini* in **Windows**.)

Storage media can also be initialized, in which case all the previous **data** is erased, and a new set of initial **formats** is put onto the disk. This should only be done if there is no need to save the earlier data.

Inkjet printer

A **dot-matrix printer** that literally applies a tiny jet of colored ink to paper. In this it is the same as traditional color printing, in which a pattern of red, green, blue, and black dots creates the impression of continuous color. Inkjet printers are cheap to buy but expensive to run and can end up costing about ten times as much to operate as a **laser printer**.

Install

To add something. The term is usually used for installing **programs** on a **hard drive**. It can also be used to mean installing additional drives or **memory** in the **hardware** of the **computer**. (*See also:* **InstallShield**.)

InstallShield

A way of **installing programs** in the **Windows operating system** that keeps them separate from all other programs. It also allows the program to be uninstalled easily.

Interface

Something that connects two completely different **systems**. A **graphical user interface**, for example, makes it possible for people to interact with the **computer** by means of familiar pictures, while the machine uses only numerical information.

Internet

A global system of **computers** connected in such a way that any user can have **access** to any other computer (unless it is protected). Now often referred to simply as the Net. It was begun in 1969 by the U.S. government's Advanced Research Projects Agency (ARPA) and was called the ARPANet. Its purpose was to allow research laboratories, universities, and libraries to share information. One of its main strengths

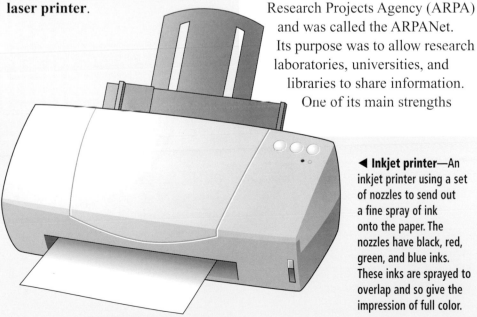

◄ **Inkjet printer**—An inkjet printer using a set of nozzles to send out a fine spray of ink onto the paper. The nozzles have black, red, green, and blue inks. These inks are sprayed to overlap and so give the impression of full color.

was that messages could be routed between two computers through any other computer in the **network**, so that if one part of the network was disabled, the rest would keep working. This ability interested the military, but the Net continued to develop far beyond the imagination of its creators. It is now a public, cooperative network stretching across the world and owned by no single country or business.

The growth of Internet traffic has enormously increased the demand for telephone lines and satellite links because every communication by Internet requires a telephone connection at least as far as the Internet Service Provider (**ISP**).

The Internet uses a set of **protocols** called **TCP/IP** (transmission control protocol/Internet protocol).

One of the most widely used functions of the Internet has been for **e-mail**. It has dramatically reduced the need for businesses to mail letters and send faxes, while speeding up the transfer of information.

The World Wide Web (www, or the **Web**) is the other main use of the Internet. Its special advantage is the use of **linked text**, called **hyperlinks**, which allows a user to jump at the click of a **mouse** from one place on a **web page** to a connected page somewhere else.

Hyperlinks can also be in the form of buttons or **images**. The **cursor** pointer turns into a pointing hand when it is over a hyperlink.

Moving from page to page randomly on the Web is called **surfing**. The two most popular Internet **browsers** are **Netscape** and **Internet Explorer**.

(*See also:* **Address**; **B2B**; **Backbone**; **e-business**; **FTP**; **Host**; **IP address**; **Ping**; **Search engine**; **UNIX**; **URL**; **Web site**.)

Internet Explorer

A **browser** for public access to the **Internet**, produced by the Microsoft Corporation. Along with **Netscape**, it is one of the two main web browsers. (*See also:* **Bookmark**.)

Intranet

A private **network** used within a business or other institution. It works like the **Internet**, but is connected only to other computers on its own network. It does not connect directly to the Internet, although there may well be a **gateway computer** that does allow **access** to the Internet as well. It is also called a **LAN** (local area network).

IP address
Internet protocol address

A 32-**bit** number that identifies each sender or receiver of information. It is like a self-addressed envelope. It is sent with the packets of information that move over the **Internet**.

The Internet **protocol** adds the sender's IP address to every message (just as a letter you send has your name and address at the top). At the receiver's **computer** the information requested is supplied, and the IP address of the sender is added, so that the message can be sent back correctly.

There are two parts to an IP address: One identifies the **network** on the Internet, and the other identifies a particular computer on that network. Only the network part of the address is needed until the packet of information gets to the user's network (just as the post office only looks at the country part of an airmail letter address until it reaches the destination country).

The Internet connects many different networks. Its protocol contains the rules that organize the way in which the packets of information are moved around. To be part of the Internet, a network needs an Internet network number, which it can request from the Network Information Center (NIC). It is the unique network number included in any packet of information sent out of the network onto the Internet.

The second part of the IP address is called a **host** number. It tells the network the name of the computer.

All this information is packaged into four decimal numbers, each representing eight bits. Each packet of information is separated by a period. But, since the string of numbers is hard to remember, the number often is represented by words called the **domain name**.

ISDN
Integrated services digital network

A **digital** telecommunications line that can transmit both voice and digital data as fast as 128 **kilobytes** per second (as opposed to a fast **modem**, which operates at 56 kilobytes per second). It is also much faster than high-speed **analog** modems (*see:* **Dial-up**).

The next step in getting faster communications will be asymmetric digital subscriber line (**ADSL**). (*See also:* **B-channel**.)

ISP
Internet service provider

A company whose main purpose is to provide **access** to the **Internet**. Some ISPs also offer games, news, and other kinds of information, but that is not their main role. There are now many free ISPs that have no connection charges and make their money partly from sharing the cost of the phone bill and partly from selling advertising space on their **home page**. (*See also:* **Access provider**; **POP**; **Roaming service**.)

J

Java

A programming language designed for use on any **computer operating system**. It was set up to build **programs** that work over the **Internet** and to make it possible for **web sites** to be more interactive. It is similar in appearance to **C++**. (*See also:* **Bean**.)

JavaScript

A reduced version of **Java**. It is called a script language (Java is a compiled language: harder to learn, but more powerful).

JavaScript is easier to learn and use than Java. It is designed to run small **applications** on the **Web**, for example, opening a new window when the user clicks a button, making a button **rollover**, or producing a random **image** whenever a user returns to a **home page**.

JPEG, JPG
Joint photographic experts group

Pronounced JAY-peg, it is a form of **compressed image** that allows the user to choose the quality of the compressed result. It is the main **format** used for photographic images on the **Web**. JPEG file names end in *.jpg*. (*For examples of JPEG format see page 23*.)

Junk e-mail, spam

The business of sending unwanted advertisements and other messages to large numbers of people through the **e-mail** system. It is the same as sending junk paper mail. Its advantage is that it can be deleted without even being opened.

Spam messages are a particular cause of concern if they have **attachments**, because they can readily transmit **viruses**. The best advice for dealing with spam is: If you didn't ask for it, and it has an attachment, trash it without even opening it, or the result could be a **computer** crash.

The word "Spam" is a trademark for a type of canned meat that was distributed widely during World War II.

K

Keyboard

The part of a **computer** that allows the user to enter letters, numbers, and other characters. It is an input-only **device**. Keyboards often contain shortcut keys, keys for moving the **cursor**, and a button for starting up and shutting down the computer. The arrangement of keys on the keyboard varies from country to country, but is similar to that on a typewriter.

Users of keyboards must be aware that continued typing can cause repetitive stress injuries. So, they should not use keyboards for extended periods, but take a break from time to time. (*See also:* **Port**.)

Killer app

An extremely successful **application** program. It may be something like the word-processing application that made many people give up typewriters and buy **computers**, or it may be a **web browser** that gets people to move onto the **Internet**.

Kilobyte (K, KB or Kb)

A unit of **memory** size or **data** equivalent to 1,204 **bytes**. (*See also:* **Gigabyte**; **Megabyte**; **Terabyte**.)

L

LAN
Local area network

A **network** of interconnected **PCs** that are directly connected to one another, for example, by **ethernet**

cabling. The LAN can have a number of independent **computers** connected to it, or it can consist of a **server** that contains all of the **programs** that are **accessed** by other computers on the LAN. One of its main advantages is **file sharing**, allowing one person (with permission) to work on files stored on another person's computer. (*See also:* **AppleTalk** and **Intranet**.)

Laptop computer, notebook computer, portable computer

A battery-powered personal **computer** designed to be portable and self-contained. It is usually about 5cm thick and about the size of a small briefcase. It is lightweight, yet still has the power of a **desktop computer**.

The small components and **circuits** needed to fit inside a laptop, together with the **active matrix display**, make it more expensive than a desktop computer of the same performance.

Laptop computers will, in general, "dock" with a cradle on a desktop computer, thus allowing them to use full-sized **monitors**, and so on. (*See also:* **Trackball**.)
(*For an illustration see page 30.*)

▼ **Keyboard**—This is a full keyboard, including keys across the top that give shortcut commands.

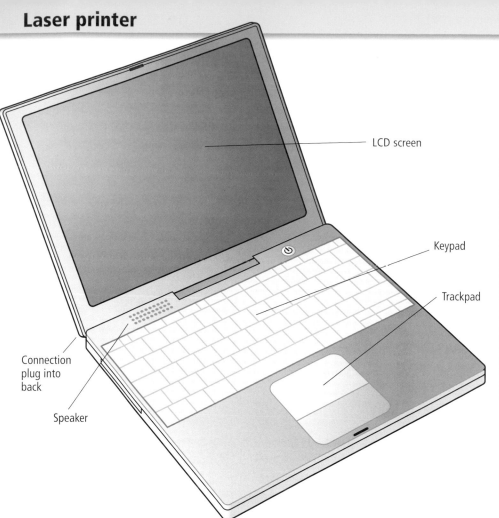

LCD screen

Keypad

Trackpad

Connection plug into back

Speaker

◀ **Laptop computer**—A portable computer called a laptop because it is designed to be used by people on their laps when traveling.

Link, linked

The way in which a word or an **image** can be used to connect one **document** with another on the same, or different, **web pages**. It can also be called a **hyperlink**. On a screen linked words are either in a different color from other text or are underlined.

Linux

A **computer operating system** similar to the **UNIX** operating

▼ **LCD, LCD display**—A display produced by using a sheet of liquid crystals. Its advantage is the smaller footprint taken up. LCD screens also use much less power than cathode-ray screens.

Laser printer

A **printer** that uses a laser beam to draw the contents of a page onto a specially coated drum in patterns of static electrical charge (the sort you get when you rub a balloon against a sweater). Once the drum is charged, it is rolled against a dry powder called toner. The toner is attracted to charged parts of the drum. The drum then presses against a sheet of paper, and the toner is transfered onto the paper. The toner is sealed into the paper using heat and pressure rollers. The drum is then discharged so that it can take up a new pattern of charge to represent the next page to be printed. Laser printers can print in black or color, although color laser printers are expensive.

Most laser printers have resolutions between 600dpi (dots per inch) and 1,200dpi. They produce a precision far higher than an **inkjet printer**.

LCD, LCD display

Some organic compounds partially melt and act like liquids at certain temperatures, but still retain some features of being a solid, in particular by behaving as crystals. **Displays** that use these materials are called liquid crystal displays.

The direction of the crystal can be affected by applying an electric current. As the crystals change direction, they change the amount of light they transmit.

The liquid crystals are influenced by a very fine grid of electrodes laid over the liquid crystal so that each tiny system on **mainframe** computers, but available for **desktop computers**. It is free. Independent programmers are encouraged to provide **add-ons** and develop the operating system further. It was developed by Linus Torvalds at the University of Helsinki, Finland. Linux has a **graphical user interface** (GUI).

Logon, login

Connecting to a remote **operating system** on the **Internet**. To log in, the user needs an ID (identification name) and a **password**. (*See also:* **Authentication**.)

M

Mac, Macintosh

The computers manufactured by Apple Computer Inc. The Macintosh is usually called simply

piece of the **screen**—a **pixel**—can be influenced independently. The actual influence is achieved by using a thin transistor placed directly at the pixel location. It creates the so-called **active matrix display** used on most modern LCD displays.

The actual result of changes to liquid crystals is a switching on and off of light, thereby producing black and white spots. They are turned into color by grouping the pixels into threes and covering each with a red, green, or blue filter.

LCD displays consume little energy and take up little space. They are more expensive than cathode-ray displays and cannot be seen from such a wide angle or in high surrounding light conditions.

the Mac. It was first manufactured in 1984 and was the first popular personal **computer** with a **graphical user interface** (GUI).

Much of the user-friendliness came from ideas originally developed at the Xerox laboratories in the 1970s, including the **mouse**.

The Macintosh was first built in a case together with a tiny 9-inch **monitor**. However, at that time it represented a major advance over the unintuitive and clunky systems otherwise available. It was an instant success that forced Microsoft to adopt many of the Mac's innovations when changing from **DOS** to the first **Windows operating system** for **PCs**.

The Macintosh has its own operating system, Mac OS, now called Version X. It runs on PowerPC **microprocessors**, developed jointly by Apple, Motorola, and IBM. The innovative iMac is a recent return to the all-in-one pattern of the original, but this time with a colorful case. The iBook is a **laptop** with a similarly striking design. iMac provides the Mac technology and interface in a low-cost package.

Macs continue to be the preferred option for people needing a highly graphic interface, while PCs are still used by people in offices dominated by needs for rapid calculations and **word-processing**, rather than design and **multimedia**.

(*See also:* **Alias** and **AppleTalk**.)

Macro

A miniprogram designed to do a specific task that is commonly required.

Mainframe

A large central business or institutional **computer**. It can

support many **terminals** and supply large amounts of computing power. Mainframes are now often called **servers** because they sit at the center of **networks**, servicing the large number of terminals or other computers connected to them. (*See also:* **UNIX**.)

Megabyte (MB or Mb)

A unit of **memory** size or **data** equivalent to a million **bytes**. (*See also:* **Gigabyte**; **Kilobyte**; **Terabyte**.)

Megahertz

(*See:* **Clock speed**.)

Memory

The part of the computer where information is stored. It can be in the form of short-term memory, **RAM** or permanently stored read-only memory, **ROM**.

(*See also:* **Cache**; **DIMM**; **Motherboard**; **SIMM**.)

Meta

Meaning "fundamental." Meta tags (<META>) in **HTML** contain basic information about a **web site** or page, such as the content type and the target audience.

Microchip, microprocessor

Often called simply a **chip**, it is at the heart of all **computers**. It consists of one of more miniaturized **circuits** etched into a piece of pure silicon wafer (hence the name chip). Uses of chips include **program** logic and **computer memory** (**RAM**).

A microprocessor performs arithmetic and logic operations such as adding, subtracting, and moving numbers from one place to another.

(*See also:* **CPU**; **IC**; **Motherboard**; **RISC**.)

MIDI
Musical instrument digital interface

A **protocol** designed for recording and playing back music on **digital** synthesizers (electronic musical instruments, typically operated by a keyboard that can produce a wide range of sounds). It does not represent sounds (as, for example, is the case for *.wav* **files**), but only instructions on how the **computer** should resynthesize the music. It is therefore very compact. Its disadvantage is that it always sounds like artificial music.

MIME
Multipurpose Internet mail extensions

A development of the **e-mail protocol SMTP** (simple mail transport protocol) that allows the exchange of different kinds of **data files** on the **Internet**, such as **images** and audio.

By specifying the MIME type, the **server** gives information to the receiving e-mail client **computer** so that it knows which interpreter (player) to use for the data being transmitted. Thus, for example, **browsers** have players for **GIF** and **JPEG** images, **HTML** files, Real Audio, **QuickTime**, and so on.

Modem

A **device** that changes outgoing **digital** signals from a **computer** to **analog** signals that can then be sent along a standard copper telephone line. When it is receiving **data**, it operates in reverse, producing digital signals for the receiving computer. The standard modem works at speeds of up to 56Kbps (kilobits per second).

(*See also:* **Bandwidth**; **Cable modem**; **Dial-up**; **Handshaking**.)

◀ **Monitor**—The name given to the computer display and the electronics encased with it.

Monitor

Strictly, the **computer display** when housed in a separate case from the rest of the computer. As a result, integrated computers, such as iMacs and **laptop computers** do not have monitors, only displays. However, in practice the words are used interchangeably. (*See also:* **Pixel**; **Screen**; **SVGA**.)

Motherboard

The main **circuit board** inside a **computer**. It contains the **microprocessor**, **memory**, **BIOS**, and other functions.

Further circuits are added to the computer in the form of "**cards**," such as sound cards, through locations on the motherboard known as expansion slots.

The motherboard is connected to all the cards and external devices through a connection circuit called a **bus**.

Mouse

A small, hand-controlled **device** used to position the **cursor** on a **computer screen**.

The conventional mouse contains a ball that rolls around as it is pulled across a surface. The changing movement of the ball is detected by sensors that send signals through a cable to the computer. The sensors only detect relative movement, so the mouse can be picked up and put down again without any change in the position of the cursor on the screen. The mouse is the most widely used of all control devices on **desktop computers**.

(*See also:* **Port**; **Trackball**; **Tablet**.)

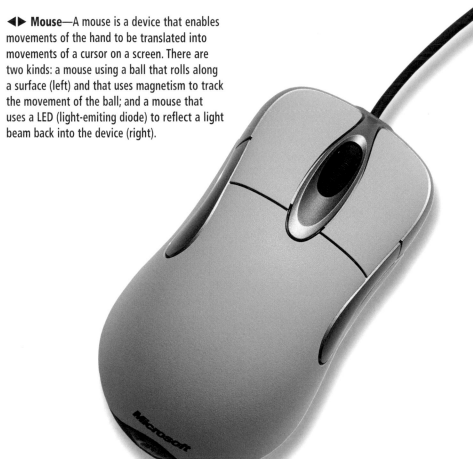

◄► **Mouse**—A mouse is a device that enables movements of the hand to be translated into movements of a cursor on a screen. There are two kinds: a mouse using a ball that rolls along a surface (left) and that uses magnetism to track the movement of the ball; and a mouse that uses a LED (light-emiting diode) to reflect a light beam back into the device (right).

Movies

The next major step in the use of **computers** is thought to involve linking camcorders and computers so that people can make their own movies and then record them onto **DVD** or cassette. Special **software** for this purpose is already readily available. (*See also:* **MPEG**.)

▼ **Movies**—The basic components for the setup for making a movie using a camcorder and computer.

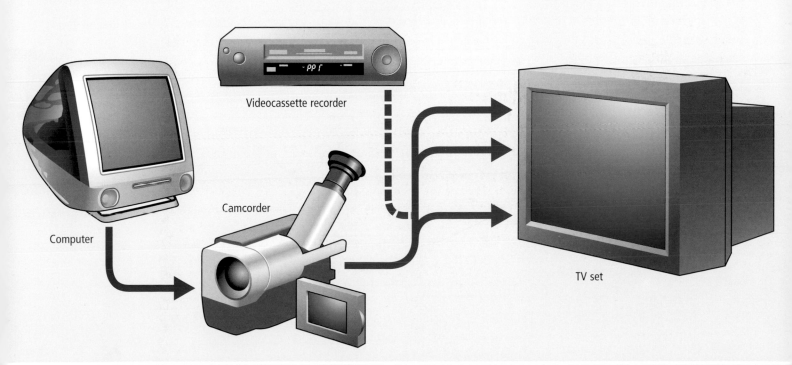

Videocassette recorder

Computer

Camcorder

TV set

MPEG
Moving picture experts group
The group that developed standards for **digital** video and digital audio **compression**.

An MPEG file (*.mpg*) is large because **movies** contain a huge amount of information.

Multimedia
A presentation that involves more than one medium, for example, sound and pictures or **text** and sound. Simple movies are not multimedia. Multimedia often features some kind of interactivity, for example, buttons to click to make other things happen.

Multimedia is most common on **CD-ROMs**, but is now finding its way onto the **Web**, as **computers** become more powerful and, in particular, as **modems** become faster.

On **web sites** motion is often produced using **MPEGs**, **QuickTime**, and Shockwave.

N

Navigation
In computing, the ability to find one's way around a **program** or a **web site** that consists of many possible combinations of paths. **Search engines** are often used to help navigation, as are **hyperlinks** and a floating window with a contents list.

Nerd
A technically adept person who has devoted time to such matters and paid less attention to social skills. (*See also:* **Geek**.)

Net
(*See:* **Internet**.)

Netscape
The name for one of the most popular **web browsers**. (*See also:* **Bookmark** and **Internet Explorer**.)

Network
A group of **computers** linked together so they can share information. Many school computers are networked so that each student can share information kept on a central computer called a **server**. In large corporations computers are linked together in networks within the business as well as with other companies.

The different types of network brought about the two terms **Internet** and **intranet**. The Internet shares information globally; an intranet shares information among computers in a local area network (**LAN**). (*See also:* **AppleTalk**; **Ethernet**; **Gateway**; **Router**.)

Newsgroup
People who discuss a topic using the NNTP (network news transfer **protocol**) and **Usenet**, a worldwide **network** of news discussion groups.

Newsgroups are organized using the first few letters of the group name as a basic classification. Examples are: news, rec (recreation), soc (society), sci (science), and comp (computers).

People can post their own ideas to the existing newsgroups, comment on what others have posted, or create new newsgroups.

The way of working with newsgroups is called "netiquette," the rules designed to keep out advertising, for example.

(*See also:* **Thread**.)

▶ **Palmtop, palm computer**—A hand-held computer designed for basic portable functions. It is halfway between a laptop and a WAP.

O

OCR
Optical character recognition
A **program** that works with a **scanner** to allow printed words to be converted into the character **codes** that a **computer** can use (**text**). The scanned **image** is analyzed for light and dark areas, and patterns are compared with the program's memory of letters and numbers. The text is then shown on the computer's **monitor**, where it can be changed as though it were an ordinary word-processing **document**.

Operating system, OS
The central **program** that manages all the other programs on a **computer**. It relates any other programs (**applications**) to the **BIOS**. These applications call on the operating system each time they need the computer to perform a task.

Operating systems (OS) can serve more than one application at a time, which is called multitasking. The main operating system for **desktop computers** is **Windows**. Others are **Mac** OS, **BeOS**, and **Linux**. All use **graphical user interfaces** (GUIs). Large computers use the **UNIX** operating system, which gets its instructions through a **keyboard**. (*See also:* **DOS**; **Platform**; **System**.)

P

Page
(*See:* **Web page**.)

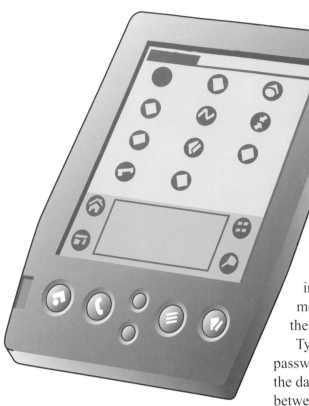

Palmtop, palm computer

The name for a very small **laptop** with built-in **display**. The term is derived from the fact that it is small enough to be held in the palm of the hand. (*See also:* **Active matrix display**.)

Parallel connector

An older sort of linkage used to connect **computers** to peripheral **devices** such as **printers** and external drives. A 36-pin connector is fitted to the device, and a thick cable connects to a 25-pin connector on the back of the computer. (*See also:* **Port**.)

Pascal

A programming language that was designed in 1967 by Nicholas Wirth to help people learn programming. Its primary use is still for instruction, since most programs today are written in **C** and C++.

Password

A string of letters and numbers required to gain **access** to **computer data**. Some passwords are publicly known (for example, typing the password "anonymous" will get you into some **programs**), but most are secret and defined by the user.

Typically, users enter a password the first time they access the data. This password (usually between four and 16 characters long and often a mixture of characters and numbers) is then held on a remote **server**. The next time the user asks for access, a small window appears asking for the password. When it is entered, it appears as a series of bullet points or asterisks, so that anyone looking at the user's **screen** cannot see it. (*See also:* **Authentication**.)

Patch

Also known as a fix, it is a small **program** designed to correct a **bug** or a deficiency in an existing program.

PC
Personal computer

The name used for most stand-alone **desktop computers**. It distinguishes them from simple computers connected to a more powerful network (**terminals**) or **mainframe** computers.

The term PC can also specifically apply to "IBM-compatible" or "**Windows**-based" personal computers. Most **Mac** owners will tell you they have a Mac, not a PC.

PCL
Printer command language

A standard printer language (set of instructions) for Hewlett Packard and compatible **printers** (mostly **PC** printers).

PCL dramatically increased printing quality in the late 1980s. It is not the same as **Postscript**, but it can usually be upgraded to Postscript with appropriate extra **software**.

pdf
Portable document format

Acrobat software produced by Adobe Systems that **compresses** information into a common **code** so that it can be read on any other **computer**, no matter what **operating system** it is using. pdf documents contain **graphics** as well as **text**, and the text retains the type style given to it by the **program** that created it. pdf files are now becoming the standard for transfering mixed graphic and text documents worldwide.

Perl
Practical extraction and reporting language

A script programming language similar to **C**. It is often used for developing **CGI** (common gateway interface) **programs** for **web sites** because it works well with **text** and can handle **binary files**.

Ping
Packet Internet or internetwork groper

An **Internet program** that lets you check that a particular Internet **address** exists. By using ping, it is possible to get the network number of the **IP address**.

▲ **Pixel**—The actual units in which information is conveyed on a display. Each pixel is in the form of a square.

Pixel

The name for the smallest block of color that can be seen on a **monitor**. All **text** and **images** are made up from pixels. As a result, the more pixels the monitor can display, the sharper and more detailed the image will appear. (*See also:* **Bit map**; **Raster graphics**.)

Platform

The underlying combination of **hardware** and **software** that provides the environment in which **applications** can run. A platform is the **operating system** together with the **program** used to coordinate how the **computer** works and the **microprocessor**. **PCs** use **Windows** platforms and often Intel **chips**, while the **Macintosh** uses the Mac OS and the PowerPC chip.

Plug-in

Small supplementary **programs** that can be **installed** to allow a particular **application** to work with special features, such as **JPEG** or **movie files**. **Web browsers** contain a raft of plug-ins, as do some other complex programs, such as Adobe Photoshop and Quark XPress. Adobe **Acrobat** is an example of a plug-in that lets the user see **documents** just as they look in print. Macromedia Flash and Shockwave for Director are examples of plug-ins for animation, and Real Audio is one of many plug-ins for sound.

PNG
Portable network graphics

A **format** for saving and **compressing graphic images**. PNG was designed to replace the older and simpler **GIF** format and the complicated **TIFF** format. PNG is easier to use between **platforms** (for example, it is easier to create an image in **Mac** OS and open it successfully in **Windows**). PNG also compresses better than GIF. PNG images do not lose quality (lossless) when they are **compressed**, unlike **JPEG** and GIF. PNG is not intended for photographic images with their large numbers of colors.

POP
Point of presence

An **access** point to the **Internet** with a unique **IP address**. **ISPs** (Internet service providers) have a point of presence on the Internet, as do **web site** owners.

POP3
Post office protocol 3

A **protocol** for receiving **e-mail**. The mail is received and held by the local **Internet server** in a location called a mailbox. As a result, users do not have to be connected to the Internet all the time. The messages waiting are **downloaded** from the Internet server by logging on to the **ISP** and then checking the mailbox.

POP3 is designed only to receive and store e-mail. A different protocol (**SMTP**) is used for sending e-mail.

Port

A socket for connecting the **computer** by wire to the **Internet** or some external **device** like a **printer**. Typical ports are **serial**, **parallel**, **ethernet**, and **USB**.

ADB (Apple desktop bus) port

Ethernet port

FireWire port

Serial ports

LocalTalk port

▲▶ **Port**—A range of ports commonly used on computers.

Portable device/ document

A piece of **hardware** that can easily be carried and so moved to work with another **computer**, for example, **storage devices**. (*See also:* **Laptop computer**.)

Portable document format (**pdf**) is designed as a portable way of moving **formated documents** between computers that use different **operating systems** (*see:* **Acrobat**).

Postscript

A programming language meant for desktop publishing packages and other sophisticated presentations. It was developed by Adobe in 1985. Postscript file names end in *.ps*.

Postscript deals with resizable (scalable) **fonts**. It can be used with any **device** that creates an **image** using dots and works with **printers** and **screen displays**. Postscript **files** can also be converted to the Adobe portable document format (**pdf**) using Adobe **Acrobat** for easy transfer between **platforms**.

The terms **laser printer** and Postscript are not the same. Cheaper laser printers use **dot-matrix** printing, rather than Postscript.

Postscript printers are the standard for **Macs** and are used with the more expensive **PCs**.

Preferences

A small **document** that holds the user's choices about how a **program** should behave. (*Compare with:* **Default**.)

Printer

A **device** that can translate text and **images** from a **computer** and print them on paper.

There are many kinds of printers now available. In general, as printers get more expensive, they work faster, use **Postscript** or color, and have a higher resolution (fineness of printing).

Some printers work like a typewriter, striking the paper through an inked ribbon (impact). In this case the letter or other character is made up of a matrix (pattern) of dots. The more dots, the less jagged the character appears. Impact printers are used when carbon copies are needed, for example, in a store where one copy of a sales receipt is kept by the customer and another is kept by the store.

An impact printer forms its image one line at a time.

Not all **dot-matrix printers** are impact printers. **Inkjet printers** are nonimpact printers that spray ink from a cartridge onto the paper as the inkjet head moves across just above the paper surface. Many of these machines print in color.

A **laser printer** is another nonimpact printer. It uses a laser beam to attract carbon powder (called toner) to a drum, which then transfers its carbon to the paper as it rolls over the drum. Most laser printers work in black and white only, although color laser printers are also available.

In general, inks for color printers are very expensive because they require several cartridges (red, green, blue, and black).

In the past printers were connected to computers using a **parallel** plug and socket. New computers use **USB** connections.

The main printer languages are Postscript and **PCL**.

Printers are supplied with a number of typefaces (**fonts**) built into their **memory chip**. Other fonts can be supplied by word-processing **software**. (*See also:* **Driver**.)

USB (universal serial bus) ports

SCSI (small computer system interface) ports

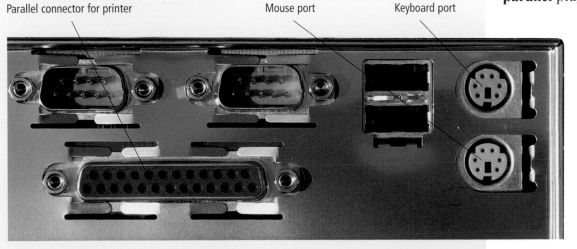

Parallel connector for printer — Mouse port — Keyboard port

Program

A set of ordered instructions telling a **computer** what operations to perform. The computer then follows these instructions one at a time, in order. Programs are the key to making a computer useful. Programs are also called **applications**.

Programs are loaded and put in storage, and the instructions are drawn on as required by the computer **operating system**.

A program is written in a computer language, for example, **C**. The statements produced make up the source program. It is translated by a **compiler** into machine **code** of 1s and 0s (*see:* **Binary**).

Programs commonly used include word-processing, spreadsheets, databases, and graphics. (*See also:* **Macro**; **Patch**; **Plug-in**; **Software**.)

Protocol

The communication language used to allow **computers** to speak to one another.

The **Internet** uses several **TCP/IP** protocols: **TCP** (transmission control protocol) rules for exchanging messages at the computer level; **IP** (Internet protocol) for exchanging messages at the Internet **address** level; and **HTTP**, **FTP**, and so on, which work with the information being exchanged.

(*See also:* **Boilerplate**; **Bug**; **Code**; **Compiler**; **Debugging**; **Encryption**.)

(*For other protocols see:* **Anonymous FTP**; **BASIC**; **C**; **COBOL**; **DHTML**; **FORTRAN**; **HTML**; **Java**; **JavaScript**; **MIDI**; **Pascal**; **PCL**; **Perl**; **POP3**; **Postscript**; **RIP—routing information protocol**; **SMTP**; **SQL**; **Telnet**; **WAP**; **XHTML**; **XML**.)

Public domain software

Programs for which the authors do not intend to claim copyright, but want anyone to be able to use the **software** free. This may or may not be the same as **freeware** because in freeware the authors retain the right to prevent anyone from altering the **code**.

Q

QuickTime

Apple Computer's system for combining sound, **text**, animation, and video in a single **file**. QuickTime files can only be viewed using a QuickTime player.

R

RAM
Random access memory
The part of the **memory** in which the **operating system**, currently active **application**, and currently used **data** are kept. RAM is stored in a **SIMM**, **DIMM**, or other memory **chip** that plugs into the **motherboard** of the **computer**. Any data in RAM can be **accessed** quickly and directly. The term random refers to the fact that although the data is not stored randomly but in a highly organized way, it can be accessed in any order.

RAM is memory that is fast but temporary. Because the computer operating system and the **programs** in use need to run as fast as they can, they are always stored in RAM. However, when the computer is switched off, the RAM clears. So, RAM is not a place for storing data more permanently—that is done on a **hard disk**.

Raster graphics

Images that are produced as a pattern or matrix of independently controlled dots, known as **pixels**. Each pixel is given a value, and that value determines its color and brightness. The **bits** that form the **code** for any image in the **computer's memory** are called a **bit map**. Raster graphics are the most common form used for

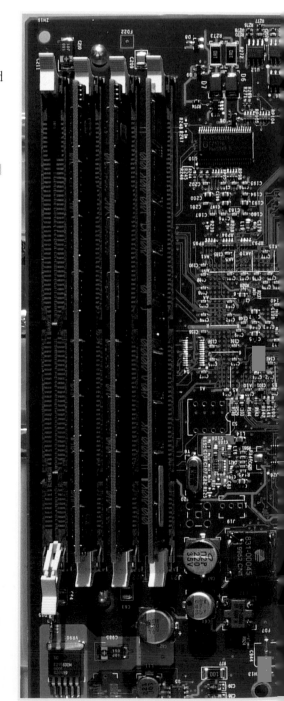

photographs displayed on computer **display screens**.

Raster graphics cannot be resized up and down; and when they are enlarged or reduced, some distortion shows as poor color or jagged edges.

RGB
Red, green, and blue
A system for representing the colors used on a **computer**

◄ **RAM**—Here you see several slots (far left) occupied by RAM cards to increase the memory of a computer.

The amount of information that a computer can hold in RAM depends on the size of its RAM. Once RAM is full, the computer starts storing data on the hard disk, and this dramatically slows down the speed at which processing can take place. Just as car enthusiasts will tell you that there is no substitute for "horsepower," computer engineers will tell you there is no substitute for RAM. That is why computer users try to buy as much RAM as they can afford for their needs.

(*See also:* **Cache**; **DRAM**; **EDO RAM**.) (*Compare with:* **ROM**.)

display. It is the same as the system used to make colors on a television screen. All transmitted colors (colors produced by beams of colored light) can be produced from red, green, and blue.

RIP
Raster image processor
Prepares **data** from a **computer** for a **printer**.

RIP
Routing information protocol
Manages information direction within a **network**.

RISC
Reduced instruction set computer
A **computer microprocessor** that is designed to perform a smaller number of some types of processing. By cutting down the number of possible tasks, or instructions, the processor can be made to work faster.

RJ
Registered jack
The type of plug-and-socket wire connector used in telephone systems and **computers** (for example, **ethernet**). Most computers are linked using the same jack as for connecting computers to an **ISDN** line. Most U.S. telephone jacks are size R11 (other countries have their own systems), so that computers using **digital** networks cannot be plugged into the (**analog**) telephone system by accident.

Roaming service
Provided by **ISPs** (Internet service providers) to allow users to **logon** no matter which state or country they might be in and still use local call charges. ISPs have cooperative agreements to

grant each other's customers local **access** to the **Internet**.

Rollover, mouseover
A technique that allows a **web page** designer to change the **images** on buttons or **text** when the **mouse** rolls over or moves over the button on **screen**. It adds to the feeling of interactivity. Rollovers are activated by **JavaScript**.

ROM
Read only memory
Memory that can be read but not changed. ROM is a permanent store of information and holds its contents even when power is turned off.

ROM chips are used for storage of the essential **software** that starts up and operates the **computer** before the **operating system** begins to take control.

(*Compare with:* **RAM**.)

Root directory
The basic **directory** of a file system off which all other directories branch.

Router
A **device** whose job is to control the direction of packets of information, looking for the least busy route to use. It is part of a **network**.

RTF
Rich text format
A **file format** designed to exchange **text** files between different **word processors** using different **operating systems**. For example, a file can be created in Word using **Windows** and sent over the **Internet** and read by a **Mac** using the Mac OS.

This system works by using only those commands and character descriptions that are common to all the major operating systems.

S

Scanner

A **device** for capturing **images** either from a page, a photo, or a transparency. Most scanners have a flat plate of glass on which the material to be scanned is placed. They are called flatbed scanners. Professional-quality scanners use a drum instead of a plate, and the material being scanned is taped on the drum.

The quality of the image displayed on a **computer screen** after scanning depends on the resolution of the scanner (the number of dots per inch for which the scanner gathers information).

Scanners work by moving a fluorescent tube across the material to be scanned and then reading the light reflected (or in the case of transparencies, transmitted) using a set of light-sensitive electronic devices known as LEDs.

Color scanning can be done in one pass or three passes of the fluorescent tube, each adding detail and quality.. (*See also:* **OCR** and **TWAIN**.)

Screen

In a **desktop computer** system using a cathode-ray tube, it is the front of the tube on which an image is displayed. The size of the screen is measured from one corner to the opposite corner (diagonally). Most screens are now at least 15 inches, with 17 and 19 inches common, and 21 inches the standard for professional **computer graphics** work. Screens are not generally measured in metric sizes.

(*See also:* **Display**; **LCD display**; **Monitor**; **Screen saver**; **SVGA**.)

▶ Screen—The front of a computer monitor.

Screen capture, screen dump

A way of making a snapshot of the information displayed on the **screen** of a **computer**.

Screen saver

A moving **image** that appears on a **screen** when the **computer** has been idle for a short time. It is designed to keep a single stationary image from remaining on the screen for a long time because that can damage the phosphors on the screen (something called screen burn). **Windows** has built-in screen savers. Many commercial and free screen savers are also available.

SCSI
Small computer system interface

Pronounced scuzzy, it is an older system for connecting **computers** to external **devices** such as **hard drives**, **printers**, **scanners**, and so on. It was developed by Apple Computer but has now been replaced by **USB** interfaces. (*See also:* **Port**.)

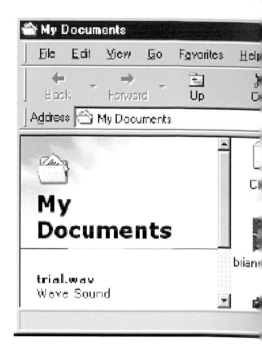

▲ Screen capture, screen dump—Any part of the screen or all of the screen can be captured. This is an active screen capture in Windows 98. To do a screen capture in Windows, press the "print scrn" key. This will put the contents of the screen onto the clipboard. Capturing the active window is achieved by pressing the "alt" and "print scrn" keys together. In Mac OS press "command," "shift," and "3" for the entire screen and "command," "shift," and "4" to be able to drag a cursor across the screen to capture the bit you want. This produces a SimpleText file on the hard disk, which can then be opened and used as required.

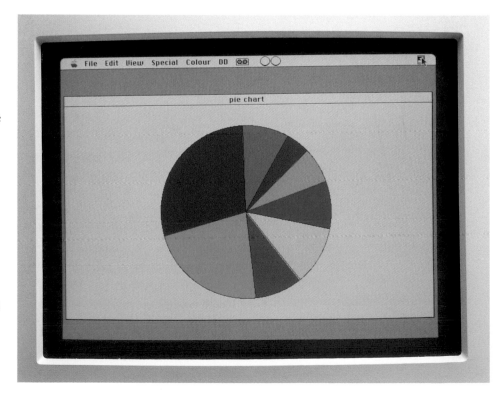

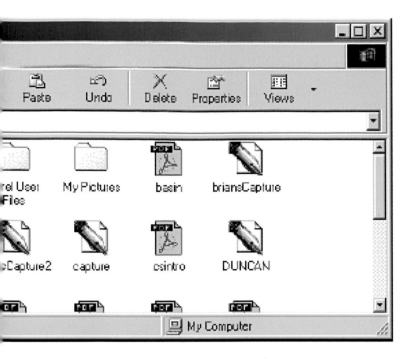

Search engine

A **program** provided by some companies for looking through the billions of **web pages** on the **Internet**. A search engine has to contain a **spider** or **crawler**, which visits all pages on the **Web** (on invitation) and creates a **hyperlink** from the search engine to that page. The search engine must also contain a powerful indexing program, or catalogue, that can display all the pages that are relevant to a user's query (as in AltaVista).

There are other ways to present Internet information. Yahoo, for example, also uses a system of structuring by topic the pages it knows about.

It is believed that no search engine currently **accesses** more than 15% of the Internet, so it is always worthwhile trying a number of search engines when researching a topic. Nevertheless, the number of pages available to all search engines can be huge.

Serial connector

Serial means one at a time. Serial connectors transfer **data** in sequence and are slower than **parallel connectors**, which allow data to be sent along several paths at the same time. **Keyboard** information is sent to a serial interface because typing creates information slowly. The **printer**, on the other hand, is connected by a parallel interface because it handles much more information. (*See also:* **Port**.)

Server

A **computer program** housed inside a computer (also itself often called a server) that provides services to other computer programs.

A **web** server provides the **web pages** that have been requested. A web client is the program that requests the web page.

The server can be located anywhere in the world; the client is the machine you make the request from and its program. (*See also:* **CGI**.)

Shareware

A low-cost way of distributing **applications** for users to try out. If users like the application, they are asked to pay for it.

Sometimes shareware can only be used for 30 days before it is disabled, or the shareware version has fewer features than the full-cost version.

SIMM
Single in-line memory module
A **RAM** (random access memory) **chip** on a **circuit board** that can be plugged into the **motherboard**. SIMMS are added to increase the amount of RAM that a **computer** has available. (*See also:* **DIMM**; **Memory**; **ROM**.)

Site
Also called a **web site**, it is a place on the **Internet** where a number of **files** are placed so they can be **accessed** by users of the World Wide **Web**. A web site is accessed through an **address**, such as *http://www.grolier.com*.

The first file to be accessed on a site is the index file (*index.html*). It then gives instructions on how to load the other files that the user might need. The first page to come up on the **screen** is called the **home page**.

Skunkworks
A small team of people who work together to develop new ideas and products. It is believed that the term originated from the fact that these people get so excited about their project that they forget to see much sun or soap!

SMTP
Simple mail-transfer protocol
A **TCP/IP protocol** used for sending **e-mail**. Its job is to stack up sent messages at the location from where they are sent all at once when the user connects to a **server**. It normally works with other protocols such as **POP3**, which save the queued messages on a server in a mailbox. (*See also:* **MIME**.)

Snail mail

Used to describe mail service: paper, envelope, and stamp. It was coined by people who regularly use instant message transmission by **e-mail**.

Software

Programs used to operate **computers**. **Hardware** is the physical machinery of the computer itself. (*See also:* **Beta test**; **Platform**; **Virus**.)

(*For examples of software see:* **Abandonware**; **Acrobat**; **Add-on**; **Freeware**; **Plug-in**; **Antivirus**; **CAD**; **Freeware**; **Public domain**.)

Source code

The **computer code** that makes something happen. You can easily see the source code written for each page on the **Web** by using a **browser**. It will **display** the **HTML** code for the **web page**.

Spam

(*See:* **Junk e-mail**.)

Speakers

Computers often have a built-in speaker designed to allow simple sounds such as alerts to be played. However, most multimedia material requires more sophisticated speakers to match sound cards with stereo capability. A wide range of speakers is now available, some with hi-fi quality, but most in simple plastic housings.

Spider

A **program** that visits **web sites** in order to read and catalogue their pages so that the details can be added to a **search engine**. Spiders are also known as **crawlers** and bots.

SQL

Structured query language

A programming language designed to retrieve and update information held in a **database**.

Storage, storage device, storage media

Anything that holds **data**, such as a **hard disk**, a **diskette**, a **Zip drive**, or a **CD-ROM**. (*See also:* **CD-R**; **CD-RW**; **DAT**.)

Streaming audio, video

Audio or video that is sent as a sequence of compressed packets of sound or **images** over the **Internet**. It requires special player **programs** designed to uncompress the **data** being received. The player is able to receive the packets and begin to play them without having to wait for all the packets to be **downloaded**. When the packets have been played, they are discarded, so the streaming audio or video does not consume huge amounts of disk space.

Supercomputer

A very powerful **computer** that uses all the latest technology for speed and storage. Supercomputers are used for science and engineering work that requires very large amounts of **data** or of calculation. For example, models for predicting climate change and

◄ **Speakers**—Most modern computers with sound cards can handle stereo sound, and so speakers are normally sold in pairs.

those used by short-term weather forecasters run on supercomputers.

Supercomputers contain multiple computers that perform parallel processing.

Supercomputers are tens of thousands times faster than a **desktop computer**.

Surf

To randomly explore the **web sites** on the **Internet**.

Surge protector, surge suppressor

A small **device**, often looking like a large plug or small box, that sits between the **computer** and the wall socket, and catches any "spikes" in the electricity voltage that might cause damage to the computer. Such spikes can momentarily reach several hundred volts, compared with the normal voltage of 120V in North America and 240V in most other countries.

SVGA

Super video graphics array

A name for a type of **display**. An SVGA display can show up to 16 million colors depending on the video memory of the **computer**. A range of **screen** resolutions can be supported depending on the screen size. Small SVGA **monitors** (say, 14 inches diagonally) display 800 **pixels** horizontally by 600 pixels vertically. The largest monitors (say, 22 inches diagonally) can display 1,800 by 1,400 or more pixels.

The dot pitch (related to the size of the phosphor dots and the holes in the screen mask, or grill, that lets the light through) is an important measure of the clarity of the screen. In general, the smaller the dot pitch, the sharper the **image**. A 0.28mm grill pitch produces an average sharpness, with 0.24mm making a sharper image.

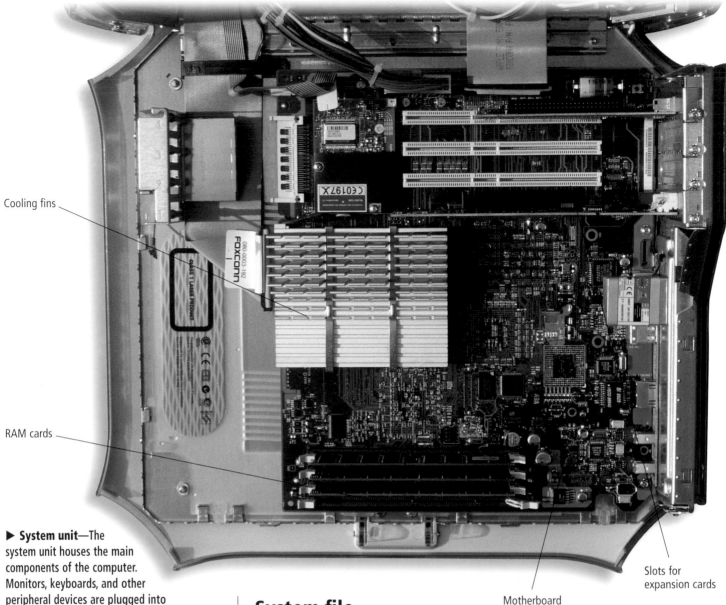

Cooling fins

RAM cards

Motherboard

Slots for expansion cards

▶ **System unit**—The system unit houses the main components of the computer. Monitors, keyboards, and other peripheral devices are plugged into it. The main circuitry is housed on a printed circuit board called a motherboard. The system unit case also houses such items as hard drives, CD players, readers and writers, DVDs, Zip drives, and floppy disk drives.

System

Short for **operating system**. The operating system manages the **programs** that run on the **computer**. In the **system file** or folder on a computer you can find all of the components that make the computer operate, together with the instructions supplied by programs. Components in a system file or folder include control panels, **fonts**, and **extensions**. Operating systems include **Windows**, **Mac**, and **Linux**.

System file

Any one of the **files** stored on the **computer** that is an essential part of making the **operating system** work. (*See also:* **System**.)

System unit

The name given to the part of the computer system that most people think of as the **computer**. It contains the **motherboard**, **RAM**, **hard disk**, and all of the central **hardware** and **software** needed to make the computer system work. It is connected to other parts of the computer system, such as the **keyboard**, **mouse**, and **monitor**, by means of **ports**, or sockets, located on the rear of the case. (*See also:* **Tower**.)

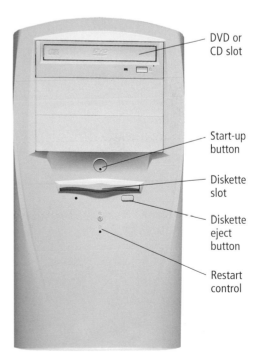

DVD or CD slot

Start-up button

Diskette slot

Diskette eject button

Restart control

T

Tablet

A flat **device** used for controlling the position of the **cursor** on the **display screen**. A tablet consists of a flat plate, together with a penlike device called a stylus. The tablet surface corresponds to the screen, and as the stylus is moved over the tablet surface, the cursor moves. It is an absolute positioning device, unlike the **mouse** or **trackball**, which are relative positioning devices.

Artists commonly use tablets because the stylus feels like a paintbrush, and they can easily alter the width of a line by changing the pressure on the stylus.

TCP/IP
Transmission control protocol/ Internet protocol)

The communication language used by **computers** over the **Internet**.

TCP/IP splits the outgoing message into packets and adds the **address** of the computer sending the message and the address of the computer due to receive the message (like enclosing a letter in an envelope, then adding the address). They are then sent over the Internet. At the receiving location TCP/IP reassembles the packets into the original message.

By splitting the message into tiny packets, many messages can be sent at the same time. That is more efficient than sending complete messages.

The **Web's HTTP** (hypertext transfer **protocol**), **FTP** (file transfer protocol), **Telnet**, and **SMTP** (simple mail transfer protocol) all use TCP/IP.

Telnet

A **protocol** for accessing a remote **computer**. While **HTTP** or **FTP**

allows you to visit and see **files**, and even **download** them, they do not let you logon to a remote computer and alter things within it, which Telnet does.

10 BASE-T ethernet

The slower, but most commonly used, form of **ethernet** connection between **computers** in the same building. It is used as a **LAN** (local area network). 10 BASE-T ethernet systems are also called "thinnets," because the cable is thin, and "cheaper nets" because the system costs less than the faster 100 BASE-T ethernet.

Terabyte

A unit of **memory** size or **data** equivalent to a thousand billion **bytes** (a thousand **gigabytes**). (*See also:* **Kilobyte** and **Megabyte**.)

Terminal

An **access device** to a **computer** system. It is normally associated with a computer **network** on which each user connects to the main computer through the terminal rather than having an independent computer of their own.

1. Dumb terminal. A **screen** and **keyboard** with no intelligence of its own that is connected to a main computer and used for simple **data** entry and retrieval.
2. Intelligent terminal. One that is part of a larger system and uses a main computer for storage of data, but has its own processing capability.

Text

In computing **data** in a written form. It contrasts with another broad term, **graphic**. Any illustration is referred to as a graphic, while any kind of word is referred to as text. Text is not referred to as "words" in

a computer context. (*See also:* **ASCII**.)

Thread

A message posted to a **newsgroup** and replies to it. Any new contributor can read the messages posted and so "follow the thread" of what is happening.

TIFF
Tagged image file format

A widely used **format** for exchanging **raster** (**bit-map**) **images** between **applications**. It is very suitable for exchanging photographic or paintinglike images, for example, those imported by a **scanner**. (*For examples of TIFF format see page 22.*)

Tower

The name for a **computer system unit** that is taller than it is wide. The purpose of a tower is to allow more room for the installation of special features such as extra computer **cards** and more **hard drives**.

▲ **Tower**—A tower has the system unit in a box that is taller than it is wide.

Address: @ http://www.science-at-school.c

Trackball

A **device** for controlling the position of a **computer cursor**. In the trackball the ball is uppermost and is directly moved by the fingers (as opposed to a **mouse**, in which the ball is face down and is moved by its casing). A trackball is often used in **laptop computers**.

Trojan horse

A **program** that hides inside an innocent-looking piece of **data** but whose purpose is to destroy the data on the **host computer**. It is a form of **virus**. The name comes from an ancient Greek story.

TWAIN

A **program** designed to allow an **image** to be scanned into a **computer** (*see:* **Scanner**). TWAIN aids direct scanning without having to open a special program.

U

UNIX

An **operating system**. It is **freeware** and written in **C** language.

UNIX operating systems are used mainly in **mainframe computers** and **servers**. UNIX was the key to the development of the **Internet** because of its robust structure and ease of use, and most Internet servers are run with a UNIX operating system. The **Linux** operating system is based on UNIX.

Upload

The process of sending **data** from a **computer** to a remote **server**, such as when adding **web pages**. (*Compare with:* **Download**.)

▲ **URL**—The electronic address of a web site.

URL
Uniform resource locator

The **address** of an **HTML web page**. The URL begins with the name of the **protocol** that is to be used, for example, **HTTP**, then the **domain name**, and possibly a **file** name. For example:

http://www.grolier.com

This is the **home page** of the **domain**. Its full address is:

http://www.grolier.com/index.html

The part after the "/" is the file name. However, it is assumed that the "*/index.html*" will be the file chosen unless something else is stated, and so it is usually not included.

A URL including a file name might be:

http:/www.curriculumvisions.com /mountain

where "*/mountain*" is the file or folder to be used.

USB
Universal serial bus

A special form of connection between the **computer** and external **devices** that allows them to be added or removed from the computer without shutting the computer down. This is known as "plug and play." Thus it is possible to plug a **Zip drive** into a USB connection and copy **data** from a computer, then pull out the USB plug and move the Zip drive to another computer without shutting down either of the computers.

USB has become a common standard for both **PCs** and **Macs**. USB can transfer data at a speed

of 12Mbps (megabits per second). (*See also:* **Port**.)

Usenet

An enormous collection of messages on a huge range of subjects that are posted on **servers** for anyone to look at and add to. Each subject is called a **newsgroup**.

V

Vector graphics

An **image** made up of a collection of points, lines, and arcs. They are created using drawing **applications**, such as those used for architectural and technical drawing. They are widely used by **computer graphic** artists. Final artwork is often a combination of vector and **raster graphics**. (*For examples of vector and raster graphics see pages 22 to 23.*)

Virtual

An imaginary presence. Virtual hosting, for example, is a service offered by companies that **host** their **web site** so that the company does not have to manage its own **server**. Virtual hosts are web space providers.

Virtual memory

Memory that is really part of a **hard disk**, but is used as though it were **RAM**. (*See also:* **Cache**.)

Virus

A piece of **computer code** that hides inside or is attached to some ordinary code, but which is designed to be spread automatically among many computer users. Viruses are usually meant to cause damage. They commonly come in **attachments** to an **e-mail**, from **downloading** infected files over the **Internet**, from a **diskette**, or from a **CD-ROM**. Some viruses are very specific to the software they infect. For example, macro viruses infect the Microsoft Word **application**.

The spread of viruses has resulted in the growth of an **antivirus software** industry.

(*See also:* **Trojan horse** and **Worm**.)

von Neumann, John

One of the 20th-century pioneers of computing, von Neumann (1903–1957) had the idea that the **computer's program** and **data** could be kept in a **memory**. Before this people had only fed programs and data into a computer while it was working. They had no means of **storage**.

W

WAP

Wireless application protocol

Designed to allow portable devices such as mobile phones to **access** the **Internet** via wireless signals.

WAP is designed to bridge the gap between people on the move and their need to access information in the same way as from their desktop or home.

WAP is a global standard that sets out the framework by which manufacturers can design their equipment. It is not controlled by any single company.

One of the key elements in WAP technology is the development of a microbrowser, a slimmed-down version of a standard browser. The microbrowser does not need the

same amount of memory as a standard browser. In order to work, the information supplied to the microbrowser by code has to be much more rigorous than the information currently supplied to most traditional browsers, as in XHTML.

These changes have happened because mobile users are no longer prepared to accept relatively basic functions from their telephone and want a mobile communications center instead.

To get this level of service, communications to mobile centers have to use a broader **bandwidth**, meaning they have to be able to transmit and receive more information at the same time.

The main issues concern the size of mobile phones, how to provide suitable power supplies, how to provide a big enough display size, how to fit enough processing power into a hand-held device, and how to transmit such huge amounts of **data**.

News, weather, and travel (including providing users with a local map so they can find their destinations) are some of the areas in which WAP will provide services for mobile users. (*See also:* **Active matrix display**.)

Wave file

Any **file** carrying sound information. Developed by Microsoft, it is the standard **PC** audio file **format**. Wave file names end in *.wav*.

Wave files can be used on **Windows** and **Mac platforms**.

Web

The millions of people and the **computers** they use to connect themselves to the **Internet** using **HTTP**. It now allows people to **access** billions of pages of

information. The most phenomenal thing about the World Wide Web is the speed with which it has revolutionized many things that people do, such as searching for information. It has given individuals the opportunity to publish electronically anything they want. It has also begun to change the way in which businesses trade via **e-business** (also called e-commerce and e-tailing).

(*See also:* **Access provider**; **Browser**; **Domain**; **ISP**; **Web page**; **Web site**.)

Webmaster

A person who manages, and often creates, a **web site** and is capable of using the **HTML code** in which web pages are written.

Web page

A basic unit of a **web site**. It can be any length and is controlled by reference to a single **HTML document**. (*See also:* **Active server page**; **Anchor**; **Applet**; **Browser**; **Cascading style sheet**; **Counter**; **DHTML**; **Frames**; **Hit**; **Home page**; **Hyperlink**; **Link, linked**; **Rollover, mouseover**.)

Web site

An organized group of **files**, written in **HTML** and including an index file that references a **home page** on the **Web**.

A web site has a **URL** that is **accessed** by a **domain** name such as *http://www.grolier.com*. This home page then leads users to other web pages.

Web sites are commonly set up by businesses, but they can also be created by individuals and have few pages. Every site begins with a home screen, no matter how large or small the site.

Because there are millions of

web sites on the Internet, one of the main problems is getting your site known. At present this is done by advertising on other sites, by linking with other sites, or by advertising in other media, such as through the mail or on radio and television. (*See also:* **Banner**; **Browser**; **Cam**; **Code**; **Cookie**; **Counter**; **Crawler**; **FAQ**; **Hit**; **Home page**; **Multimedia**; **Navigation**; **POP**; **Search engine**; **Site**; **Spider**; **Surf**; **Webmaster**.)

Windows

The name of recent **operating systems** sold by Microsoft. Windows is **installed** on most **PCs**.

Word processor

A **computer program** designed to act like an electronic typewriter, an editor, and a typesetter, allowing users to arrange their work on a page and check it for spelling and grammar. Word processors also allow **images** to be incorporated. They give the user a **WYSIWYG** (what you see is what you get) view of the material they create.

World Wide Web

(*See:* **Web**.)

Worm

A type of **virus** that can copy itself to spread across a **network**.

WYSIWYG
What you see is what you get

Pronounced whizz-ee-wig, it is part of a **program's** interface that displays a page of **text** on **screen** exactly as it will print. Almost all **word processors** and desktop publishing **software** have WYSIWYG capabilities.

X

XHTML

A transitional version between **HTML** and **XML**. It requires stricter attention to syntax than HTML but is less rigorous and easier to write than XML.

XML
Extensible markup language

A markup system similar to **HTML**, except that the markup symbols used are not limited to a predefined set. That makes it a much more flexible way of describing both the shape of the page and also the nature of its contents.

Z

Zip

A **program** designed to **compress files** for sending over the **Internet** or for **archiving**.

Zip drive

A **portable** disk drive and large **diskettes** mainly used to **backup** a **hard drive** and to transfer **data** between **desktop computers** that are not **networked**.

◄ **Web site**—A typical highly visual web site.

Index

A

Abandonware 3
Abbreviations used in chat 3
Accelerated graphics port 3
Access 3
Access provider 3
Access time 3
Acrobat 3
Acronym 3
Active matrix display 4
Active server page 4
ActiveX 4
Adapter 4
ADC 4
Add-on 4
Address 4
Adobe (see: Acrobat; pdf; Plug-in)
ADSL 4
AGP (see: Accelerated graphics port)
Alias 4
Aliasing 4
Analog 5
Analytical engine (see: Babbage, Charles; Computer)
Anchor 5
Animated GIF 5
Anonymous e-mail 5
Anonymous FTP 5
Antialiasing 5
Antivirus software 6
Applet 6
AppleTalk 6
Appliance 6
Application 6
Archive 6
ASCII 6
@ at, address sign 6
Attachment 6
Authentication 6
Autoresponder 6

B

B2B 6–7
B-channel 7
Babbage, Charles 7
Backbone 7
Backup 7
Bandwidth 7
Banner 7
BASIC 7
Baud 7
BBS 7
BCC, BC 7
Bean 7
BeOS 7
Beta test 7
Binary 8
BinHex 8
BIOS 8
Bit 8
Bit map, bitmap 8
Bit rate 8
Bit stream 8
Board (see: Circuit board)
Boilerplate 8
Bookmark 8
Boot 8
Bot (see: Crawler; Spider)
Browser 9
Bug 10
Burn 10
Bus 10
Business-to-business (see: B2B)
Byte 10

C

C++ (see: C)
C 10
Cable modem 10
Cache 10
CAD 10
Cam 10
Card 10–11
Cascading style sheet 11
CD-R 11
CD-ROM 11
CD-RW 11
CGI 12
Channel 12
Chassis 12
Chat 12
Chip 12
Circuit, circuit board 13
Clip art 13
Clock speed 13
COBOL 13
Code 13
com 13
Compiler 13
Compression, compressing 15
Computer 14–15
Computer graphics 15
Computer language (see: Protocol)
Configuration (see: Initialization)
Cookie 15
Counter 15
CPU 15
Cracker (see: Hacker)
Crawler 15
Crossover cable 15
Cursor 16
Cyber- 16
Cyberspace 16

D

DAT 16
Data 16
Database 16
Debugging 16
Default 16
Defragmenter 16
Desktop 16
Desktop computer 16
Device 17
DHTML 17
Dial-up 17
Difference engine (see: Babbage, Charles)
Digital 17
DIMM 17
Directory 17
Disk (see: Diskette; Hard disk)
Diskette 17
Display, display screen 18
DNS 18
Document 18
Domain, domain name 18–19
DOS 19
Dot-matrix printer 19
Dotcom company 19
Download 19
DRAM 19
Driver 19
DVD 19

E

e- 20
e-book 20
e-business, e-commerce 20
Electronic mail (see: e-mail)
e-mail 20
Encryption 20
End user 20
Eniac (see: von Neumann, John)
EPS (see: Format)
e-tailing (see: e-business, e-commerce)
Ethernet 20
Eudora (see: BCC)
Explorer (see: Internet Explorer)
Extension 20

F

FAQ 20
Favorite (see: Bookmark)
File 20
File sharing 21
Firewall 21
FireWire 21
Fix (see: Patch)
Floppy disk (see: Diskette)
Font 21
Foo 21
Footprint 21
Format 21, 22–23
FORTRAN 21
Fragmentation (see: Defragmenter)
Frames 21
Freeware 24
FTP 24

G

Gates, Bill (see: DOS)
Gateway 24
Geek (technofreak) 24
GHz 24
GIF 24
Gigabyte (GB or Gb) 24
Gopher 24
Graphic 24
Graphical user interface (GUI) 24
Graphics interchange format (see: GIF)

H

Hacker 24
Handshaking 24
Hard disk, hard drive 24–25
Hardware 26
Hertz (Hz) 26
Hit 26
Home page 26
Host 26
HTML 26
HTTP 26
Hub 26
Hyperlink 26

I

I/O 26
IC 26
Icon 26
Image 26–27
Initialization 27
Inkjet printer 27
Install 27
InstallShield 27
Interface 27
Internet 27
Internet Explorer 28
Intranet 28
IP address 28
ISDN 28
ISP 28

J

Java 28
JavaScript 28
JPEG, JPG 28
Junk e-mail 28–29

K

Keyboard 29
Killer app 29
Kilobit (see: Bit rate)
Kilobyte (K, KB or Kb) 29

L

LAN 29
Language, computer programming (see: Protocol)
Laptop computer 29–30
Laser printer 30
LCD, LCD display 30–31
Link, linked 30
Linux 30–31
Live cam (see: Cam)
Logon, login 31
Lovelace, Ada (see: Computer)

M

Mac, Macintosh 31
Macro 31
Mainframe 31
Megabyte (MB or Mb) 31
Megahertz (see: Clock speed; Hertz; Memory)
Memory 31
Meta 31
Microchip, microprocessor 31
MIDI 32
MIME 32
Modem 32
Monitor 32
Motherboard 32
Mouse 32–33
Mouseover (see: Rollover)
Movies 33
MPEG 34
MS-DOS (see: DOS)
Multimedia 34
Multitasking (see: Operating system)

N

Navigation 34
Nerd 34
Net (see: Internet)
Netscape 34
Network 34
Newsgroup 34
Notebook computer (see: Laptop computer)

O

OCR 34
Operating system, OS 34

P

Page (see: Web page)
Palmtop, palm computer 35
Parallel connector 35
Pascal 35
Password 35
Patch 35
PC 35
PCL 35
pdf 35
Peripherals (see: Device)
Perl 35
Personal computer (see: PC)
Ping 35
Pixel 36
Platform 36
Player (see: MIME)
Plug and play (see: USB)
Plug-in 36
PNG 36
POP 36
POP3 36
Port 36–37
Portable computer (see: Laptop computer)
Portable device/document 37
Postscript 37
PowerPC (see: Mac; Platform)
Preferences 37
Printer 37
Program 38
Protocol 38
Public domain software 38

Q

QuickTime 38

R

RAM 38–39
Raster graphics 38–39
Raster image processor (see: RIP)
Reboot (see: Boot)
Repetitive stress injury (see: Keyboard)
Resolution (see: Dot-matrix printer; Printer; Scanner; SVGA)
RGB 39
RIP (raster image processor) 39
RIP (routing information protocol) 39
RISC 39
RJ 39
Roaming service 39
Rollover, mouseover 39
ROM 39
Root directory 39
Router 39
Routing information protocol (see: RIP)
RSI (see: Keyboard)
RTF 39

S

Scanner 40
Screen 40
Screen capture, screen dump 40
Screen saver 40
SCSI 40
Search engine 41
Serial connector 41
Server 41
Shareware 41
SIMM 41
Site 41
Skunkworks 41
SMTP 41

Snail mail 42
Software 42
Sound (see: Wave file)
Source code 42
Spam (see: Junk e-mail)
Speakers 42
Speed, computer (see: Clock speed)
Spider 42
SQL 42
Storage, storage device, storage media 42
Streaming audio, video 42
Supercomputer 42
Surf 42
Surge protector, surge suppressor 42
SVGA 42
System 43
System file 43
System unit 43

T

Tablet 44
Tagged image file format (see: TIFF)
TCP/IP 44
Technofreak (see: Geek)
Telnet 44
10 BASE-T ethernet 44
Terabyte 44
Terminal 44
Text 44
Thread 44
TIFF 44
Tower 44
Trackball 45
Treeware (see: e-book)
Trojan horse 45
TWAIN 45

U

Universal serial bus (see: USB)
UNIX 45
Upload 45
URL 45
USB 45
Usenet 45

V

Vector graphics 45
Virtual 45
Virtual memory 45
Virus 45–46
von Neumann, John 46

W

WAP 46
Wave file 46
Web 46
Webmaster 46
Web page 46
Web site 46–47
Windows 47
Wireless application protocol (see: WAP)
Word processor 47
World Wide Web (see: Web)
Worm 47
WYSIWYG 47

X

XHTML 47
XML 47

Z

Zip 47
Zip drive 47